Radical Universalism

Radical Universalism
Beyond Identity

OMRI BOEHM

nyrb **New York Review Books** New York

This is a New York Review Book

published by The New York Review of Books

207 East 32nd Street, New York, NY 10016

www.nyrb.com

Library of Congress Cataloging-in-Publication Data
Names: Boehm, Omri author
Title: Radical universalism: beyond identity / by Omri Boehm.
Description: New York: New York Review Books, 2025.
Identifiers: LCCN 2025023625 (print) | LCCN 2025023626 (ebook) |
  ISBN 9781681379852 paperback | ISBN 9781681379869 ebook
Subjects: LCSH: Kant, Immanuel, 1724–1804 | Humanism | Identity
  politics
Classification: LCC B821 .B524 2025 (print) | LCC B821 (ebook)
LC record available at https://lccn.loc.gov/2025023625
LC ebook record available at https://lccn.loc.gov/20250

ISBN 978-1-68137-985-2
Available as an electronic book; ISBN 978-1-68137-986-9

The authorized representative in the EU for product safety and
compliance is eucomply OÜ, Pärnu mnt 139b-14, 11317 Tallinn, Estonia,
hello@eucompliancepartner.com, +33 757690241.

Printed in the United States of America on acid-free paper.

10 9 8 7 6 5 4 3 2 1

For Amitai

This is the Triumph of the religion of the prophets over the moral philosophy: that it alone discovered the idea of humanity.

—HERMANN COHEN

The "we" must not be previous to the question.

—MICHEL FOUCAULT

Contents

Introduction
The Origin

In 1959, W. E. B. Du Bois was invited to the Kremlin, where he was informed that a committee had chosen him as that year's recipient of the International Lenin Peace Prize. The timing was not accidental. A Soviet committee bestowed on the towering African American scholar and author of *Black Reconstruction in America*[1] a prize "for the strengthening of peace among the nations"—a sort of communist Nobel—to make a point. As the Cold War was in full swing and the Civil Rights Movement was picking up momentum, Soviet Russia presented itself as successful where US liberal democracy had failed in achieving racial justice. No doubt, there was a political agenda behind the committee's decision, but it would be mistaken to dismiss it as mere propaganda. In Jim Crow America, Du Bois could hardly have been bestowed a similar honor by the White House. The previous year, he had already received an honorary doctorate in economics from the Humboldt University of Berlin, where at the turn of the nineteenth century he had spent a brief but formative period, taking classes with figures such as August Meitzen (Max Weber's mentor) and Wilhelm Dilthey. In 1960, as the Lenin Prize was awarded at the Soviet embassy back in Washington, DC—Du Bois insisted that the ceremony would be held in America—the man who once described his life as the "autobiography of the race concept,"[2] concluded his acceptance speech with a statement that in his mouth is hardly laconic. "I still cling to the dream of the America into which I was born."[3]

Four years later, in September 1964, Martin Luther King Jr. would travel to Berlin for a historic visit, at the invitation of the city's mayor, Willy Brandt. The official reason for the invitation was commemorating John F. Kennedy, who spoke in Berlin the previous year in front of the wall and was assassinated just a few months later. Brandt's decision to honor the assassinated president of the Western superpower conqueror-turned-protector by inviting the Black and still highly controversial icon of the Civil Rights Movements was remarkable. Just the year before, King was sitting in a Birmingham cell for marching in Alabama against court orders. The publication of his "Letter from Birmingham Jail" overlaps virtually to the day with Kennedy's "*Ich bin ein Berliner.*" Clearly, West Germany also had ways to make a point about Western values and racial justice. During his visit, King insisted on crossing the wall and visiting East Berlin, despite the reluctance of his hosts. In fact, the American embassy attempted to sabotage the crossing by confiscating King's passport. In the end, he did cross and gave a short sermon in the Marienkirche, using his American Express card for identification at the border. A president of the American Academy in Berlin would comment many years later that this was one indication that "capitalism can work" after all.[4]

It may be tempting to think that the heated identity debates of the last years were eclipsed overnight by Russia's gruesome attack on Ukraine in February 2022, Hamas's brutal massacre of Israeli civilians on October 7, 2023, and Israel's systematic destruction of the Gaza Strip since. All mark the sudden return of an old-new type of conflict to the center of attention. New wars, anything but cold, are in the making, and could seem to take the attention from the debates about race, gender, and identity. But think again: Questions of racial and social justice have always haunted Western liberal democracy—with the United States of America as its blemished symbol—against challenges facing it from without. True, in contrast to Soviet Russia, Vladimir Putin does not confront the West with a thorough ideology. But for years now, he has been positioning himself as the alternative to Western liberalism with regards to gay rights, the attack on Christian family values, and ethnic "threats" posed by welcoming immigrants. That's one of the reasons why not just the president of the United States but large portions of the Republican Party count as Putin enthusiasts. Besides, it seems clear that if Putin has any ideology, it is a nihilist one, celebrating power, and the question is to what extent what people call the West stands in good faith for an alternative ideal.

This question has been reopened especially after October 7th and its aftermath that many, including the International Criminal Court and the International Court of Justice in the Hague, investigate as acts of genocide and crimes against humanity. Nothing makes the challenge to liberal democracy, broadly conceived, clearer: The strength of the principles for which we fight externally is measured by the integrity with which we hold these principles within.

For several years now, liberal democracy has been facing a crisis. The familiar intellectual attacks on its core value—Enlightenment universalism—have increasingly gained footing in political circles beyond sophisticated intellectual debates and lofty philosophy departments. What began in the 1960s as a postmodern provocation from Paris, carrying clear echoes from the Black Forest of the 1920s and '30s, now influences politics well outside America's Culture Studies departments of the 1980s. The version of postmodernism that is being exported back to Europe in the form of critical race and post- or de-colonial theory is one that does not take the dreams of a Martin Luther King any more seriously than "the dream of America" into which Du Bois was born. Those dreams are being dismissed as illusions by both the left and the right that tend to agree on at least one point: The problem with Enlightenment universalism is not so much that it has failed but that it was attempted. Indeed, both sides of the aisle strive to replace the measure of abstract universalism by concrete identity: the right fights in terms of traditional values, the left fights in the name of gender and race. Universal humanism is no longer accepted as the basis from which unjust laws and discriminatory power structures should be criticized and transformed. Rather, it is perceived as the mask that allows those in power to keep those power structures.

Authors writing in solidarity with African Americans, LGBTQ+ communities, ethnic minorities, and other discriminated groups—not to say endangered groups, like the Palestinians —often oppose the critique of "identity politics" or "postcolonialism" by presenting it as a form of "white fragility," or the hypocritical oversensitivity of the privileged. And, often, not without reason. One author went so far as to dismiss the growing talk of an "illiberal left" as a "fairy tale."[5] While it is easy to focus on "juicy anecdotes about the excesses of anti-racist leftists," the argument goes, these only constitute a "marginal phenomenon." The growing progressive anti-universalist trends are not about "locking people into a would-be prison of identity" but about "demanding fundamental rights."[6]

Especially if fundamental rights are at stake, however, the growing opposition to Enlightenment universalism, and the accompanying conviction that Immanuel Kant was the father of modern racism and even Nazism,[7] should be taken more seriously. At stake are not minor juicy anecdotes, like the firing of a *New York Times* columnist or a *New York Review of Books* editor in chief for holding views that disagree with current convictions. As we enter an epoch of fighting for Western liberal democracy in Europe, as we struggle against the rise of far right politics and ethnic nationalism, Donald Trump's attack on the rule of law and on global conventions; as we face global disasters and migration waves, it makes a difference whether we hold fast to the idea of universal humanism as a compass, even a weapon, or create a society in which this idea is mocked and despised. On October 9, 2023, I held a Kant seminar in New York, asking my students to speak, in the context of Kant and the ideal of human dignity, about Hamas's attack: Does a stateless, colonized people like the Palestinians have a right to attack Israeli civilians in this way? None of my students agreed to oppose Hamas. Some supported the act, including the rape of Israeli women ("if it had occurred"); others just said that we cannot tell a colonized people how to emancipate themselves. Up until recently, the confrontation between self-proclaimed universalists and postcolonialists or anti-Enlightenment critics could seem academic—or, worse, one that's reducible to the petty anecdotes provided by both identity politics *and* its critics. At least since October 7th, we understand the stakes.

I can imagine that some liberal universalists in the center—or those who are on the so-called pro-Israeli side—are at this point nodding their heads in agreement. That may be too fast. For many years now, what liberal democrats understand as "universalism" has been shrinking and shrinking; by now, all that remains are the concept's empty shells. The clearest indication of the void may be the disappearance of the concept of duty, and the prevalence of the concept of right. All of us are familiar with the canonization of human rights that emerged at the end of the Cold War "as the international morality of the end of history" and called for an "entire library" of literature that explains their grounds.[8] While there exists a vast literature on the history, philosophy, and sociology of rights, hardly, if ever, is the question posed whether human duties are still alive. As one classic article on the topic suggests, whereas the concept of duty is premodern and religious, the concept of right is modern and secular: Duties are what philosophers call heteronomous. Moses brought written divine duties down from Mount Sinai and *gave* them to the Hebrews. Rights, by contrast, are the mark of human self-determination

17

or autonomy.[9] In this convenient atmosphere, liberals rarely argue for some hard universal duty for all humans that may well demand that they act against their interests—it usually does. Instead, they invoke their right as citizens to refrain from doing just that. When such "universalists" in turn defend Enlightenment rationalism against "identity politics," it tends to be the positivist strand of that movement that identifies "reason" with "interests," and for which "Enlightenment universalism" is, properly understood, a contradiction in terms. It isn't surprising, therefore, that a professed anti-universalist such as Richard Rorty provides the backbone for much of the liberals' allegedly universalist worries about identity. When in the 1990s Rorty led the attack on "culture studies," he opposed the postmodern concept of identity with that of "national pride."[10] His most acute current follower, Mark Lilla, similarly confronts identity with "we-liberalism" and "patriotism," but unlike Rorty, he does hold that the alternative he thereby offers is universalist.[11] For the historian Jill Lepore, who is much more progressive than Rorty or Lilla, there is "only one way" to defend liberal universalism and that is "making the case for the nation." Whereas Rorty explicitly appealed to Avishai Margalit's liberal Zionism when speaking of American liberal patriotism, Lepore explicitly referred to Yael Tamir's liberal Zionist argument in *Liberal Nationalism*. Since she makes the case specifically for the American nation, Lepore adds, this requires "grabbing and holding onto a very good idea: that all people are equal and endowed from birth with inalienable rights."[12]

It should have been obvious that to make a case for universalism, the nation is the wrong starting point. A gulf separates the only possible origin of universalist politics—a truth about the equality of all humans—and the reduction of this truth to a "very good idea." That we have become numb to the allegedly insignificant difference between the two may be the best evidence that the meaning of universalism has been successfully shredded to pieces. It is now shredded to pieces with the anti-humanist failures, not just of the postcolonial left but of liberal progressives in the international community who have failed to uphold international law: Protect the Palestinians from Israel's systematic destruction of conditions of life in Gaza. All too often, universalists' concern about the anti-universalism of "postcolonialists" and "critical race" thinkers has been the most comfortable way to bury uncomfortable universalist commitments—the duty to prevent crimes against humanity, and even genocide. The anti-humanism of some left circles is answered with hegemonic "post-humanism," where the idea of humanity has been degraded as "metaphysical" or moral fanaticism. The call to protect international law and hold Israel, and Israeli war criminals, strictly accountable is denounced by many as "problematic" if not anti-Semitic. The thread unifying both sides of this debate has been, from the start, the willingness to tolerate, and even justify, crimes against humanity.

For those who still hope to reclaim a universalist humanism that resists both, Kant remains the indispensable thinker. He grasped that the Enlightenment movement that preceded him was not a universalist movement but, in fact, universalism's worst enemy. Its positivist reduction of humans to blind nature replaced humanity with what Nietzsche would call "wise beasts"—objects of mastery and possession, exploitation and enslavement, not dignity. It is against this reduction that Kant insisted that the concept of humanity must remain abstract: free of biological, zoological, historical, and sociological facts. Such a metaphysical idea of humanity was familiar at least since the biblical prophets; what made Kant's achievement epoch-changing was his ability to translate the biblical idea without falling back on religious faith or scientific reduction. In Kant, the idea of humanity was for the first time formulated as a moral concept: What makes humans human is not a natural characteristic but their freedom to follow their duty to moral laws. It is because human beings are open to the question of what they ought to do that they themselves are subjects of absolute dignity.

The term "absolute" is not gratuitous. By formulating the idea of humanity as a moral concept, Kant did not just translate the biblical notion of duty; he modernized the idea of following a law that is not man-made. The fate of universalism hangs together with the fate of this concept: Only a law or a truth that's independent of human convention is universal in *scope* rather than relative to the interests, identities, desires, and "good ideas" of those who have the power to legislate in human society. As we shall see, the commitment to universalist principles is often grounded in deep-rooted historical commitments—and then, as in the case of the German context, historical commitments mark the limit of universalist ones and undermine them from within. More important, only such a law is universal also in *authority* rather than just scope—it transcends the legitimacy that is conferred upon human agreements that may well be unjust. Kant would agree on this point with "identity leftists": Short of an abstract idea of humanity and a metaphysical concept of law, universalist lingo is identity politics for white men. It allows those in power to exploit the shells of an empty moral language to preserve unjust power structures that ought to be transformed.

And yet, just as fake universalists pursue their own identity politics, the identarian left shares with fake universalism more than they would like to concede. Anti-universalist theories tend to provide intellectual frameworks that deconstruct race or gender as biological concepts. Debates focus on unearthing the Enlightenment, or Kant, as the inventors of the scientific idea of race; on whether, say, Du Bois did or did not completely overcome a biological understanding of that concept; whether we should occupy ourselves only with the biological "meaning of race" or also with "the truth of it" (and, as the case may be, its falsity).[13] The tacit assumption is that by contrast to race (or gender), humanity *is* a biological concept. But it makes very little sense to deconstruct a dehumanizing concept of race while at the same time celebrating the destruction of the concept of humanity. The fight against systematic injustice and fake universalism can only be carried out in the name of true universalism. Not in the name of identity.

In the following, I offer a rereading of three texts: the Declaration of Independence, Kant's "What Is Enlightenment?," and the Binding of Isaac. This is not going to proceed as a one-text, one-chapter scholarly sort of interpretation. Rather, I make a case for universalism by studying the way in which these texts intertwine: They are monuments of a tradition that stands near to us but remains too often misunderstood; one in which the moral idea of humanity as open to absolute duty was still living.

The Declaration of Independence is the clearest political expression of that tradition. That is the reason why from pronouncing a "self-evident truth" about humans it moves by logical syllogism to asserting the right of revolution—here is one conclusion that doesn't follow from a mere "good idea." The history of modern liberalism from John Dewey to John Rawls, from Rorty to Lilla or Lepore, can be told as a story of intellectuals turning their backs on the Declaration in the aftermath of the Civil War. If this is so, liberalism as we have come to know it, or what I call fake universalism, consists in rejecting a lineage that starts at 1776, continues with the abolitionist movement, Abraham Lincoln, Gettysburg, and King, and still regards truth, not just freedom, as the driving force of the American dream.

Kant's definition of Enlightenment as "man's emergence from his self-imposed immaturity"[14] contains the foundation of the redefinition of humanity in moral rather than biological terms. Immaturity in humans can be self-imposed only because maturity, or thinking for oneself, is an *Aufgabe*, or duty, that depends on our use of our own freedom—not a development that is naturally ensured. However, as Kant and Alexis de Tocqueville both realized, thinking for oneself—rejecting the authority of others—is virtually impossible where an independent standard of justice has been replaced by human consensus. Modern liberal thinkers sometimes take pride in rejecting all independent standards and the creation of an idea of humanity that has "no room for obedience to a nonhuman authority."[15] But this allegedly democratic replacement of higher justice by sheer human authority threatens to create a tyranny of the masses that makes conformism second nature. Paradoxically, perhaps, thinking for oneself, refusing the authority of others, is only possible by following a law that is not man-made.

The Binding of Isaac will be considered here not only because that story seems to pose the greatest obstacle to the biblical tradition of obedience to a higher law but because coming to terms with that narrative is necessary to correct a lingering misconception about the origin of universalism in biblical monotheism. Nietzsche provides a powerful formulation of that misconception. "Monotheism," he writes, or "the faith in one normal god beside whom there are only pseudo-gods—was perhaps the greatest danger that has yet confronted humanity."[16] For Sigmund Freud, too, the monotheistic idea, imposed on the Jews by Moses—an Egyptian priest, he claims, not a Jewish prophet— infused into Western civilization a universalism that is, among other things, the most violent form of intolerant religion.[17] Jan Assmann analyzes this Jewish Egyptian notion as the Mosaic distinction, or as monotheism's "price": a revolutionary intellectual innovation that combined an absolute exclusive truth with religious thinking and created, among other things, violence and exclusion.[18] One way to see how these mixed views of monotheism reverberate is the idea that liberal tolerance—not just about religion but about ethics—is a progress of Western tradition from Jewish Egyptian monotheism to more tolerant polytheism.[19]

This view, however, contains a grave misunderstanding of biblical monotheism and, accordingly, of universalism. Moses is not the father of monotheism, Abraham is, and the idea that there is only one true God to the exclusion of all pseudo-deities is not monotheism's chief intellectual achievement. The main accomplishment of biblical monotheism is the affirmation of an exclusively one true God—*and then still subjecting him to a higher justice standing above him.* Only with this move is the ethical significance of monotheism, and the universal idea of humanity to which it gives rise, understood, but that innovation is completely unfamiliar to Moses—no matter whether he was Jewish or Egyptian. It is Abraham, the "father of all nations" and of the three monotheistic faiths, who confronts the only true deity: "Far be it from you to do such a thing, and slay the righteous with the wicked; shall not the judge of all the earth do what is just?"[20] There is only one true God, but the authority of universal justice stands above it.

The paradox, of course, is that the same Abraham who utters this speech receives immediately thereafter a direct divine command to sacrifice, or murder, his "only beloved son." And on a first look, he demonstrates the model of monotheistic faith by placing God's order above justice.

Kant is the first thinker in modern history who condemned Abraham's obedience. Since the duty to humanity is universal, it stands above the authority of any command—of kings or deities. We shall see that once the Binding of Isaac is properly understood, Kant's condemnation of Abraham only translates Abraham's own monotheistic innovation. The origin of universalism in mono-theism cannot be understood by reference to Freud's relation to Moses; it must be studied through Kant's relation to Abraham. His idea of humanity, and indeed of Enlightenment, is grounded in the Abrahamic distinction: Following absolute duty is not the origin of obedience but of disobedience. A law that is not man-made exists, but it remains firmly in human hands. Because humans have a duty to this law, no human ever has the right to obey. To be alienated from this right is to have human dignity and command absolute respect.

OMRI BOEHM
New York, May 2025

Acknowledgments

THIS SHORT BOOK is the result of numerous intellectual debts—to experts, colleagues, students, mentors, and friends. Some of them commented on specific topics; others on how the diverse topics (politics, philosophy, history, theology) fit together. Thanks are due to Yuval Adler, Karl Ameriks, Alice Crary, Jay Bernstein, Richard Bernstein, Avrum Burg, Thomas Cantone, Ulrika Carlsson, Michael Della Rocca, Wolfram Eilenberger, Tami Ezer, Jordi Graupera, Edward Greenstein, Karen Haber, Karsten Harries, Axel Hutter, Paul Kottman, Dan Landau, Yoni Leibowitch, Thomas Meyer, Jack Miles, Susan Neiman, Roberto Palomba, Leiki Saban, Anat Schechtman, and Sarah Schweig. Special gratitude is due to Ceciel Meiborg, who provided extensive and indispensable commentary. Eti and Amnon Boehm, my parents, provided extensive support and criticism, as did Inbal Hever, my wife, who accompanied me line by line.

The Mark of Cain

I have tried to make it clear that it is wrong to use immoral means to attain moral ends. But now I must affirm that it is just as wrong, or even more, to use moral means to preserve immoral ends. . . .

The . . . great stumbling block in the stride toward freedom is not the White Citizen's Councilor or the Ku Klux Klanner, but the white moderate, who is more devoted to "order" than to justice. . . .

"An unjust law is no law at all."

—MARTIN LUTHER KING JR., "Letter from Birmingham Jail"

1.

ON OCTOBER 16, 1859, John Brown, a white abolitionist from Connecticut, led a raid on the United States Armory and Arsenal at Harpers Ferry, in Virginia, took its guards hostage, and successfully seized the facility. He carried out the attack with twenty-three men: sixteen of them white, including three of his sons, three Black Northerners, one fugitive slave and three freed ones. Their plan was to distribute the 100,000 muskets and rifles among slaves throughout the South and start a war of emancipation. When the group took over Harpers Ferry, several of its men were already living as fugitives from justice. This status was conferred upon them due to an incident two years earlier: Along with his sons and some other men, Brown abducted five proslavery leaders in Kansas and executed them in what came to be known as the Pottawatomie Massacre.

By some measures, the Harpers Ferry insurrection failed. Early on October 18th, less than two days after the incident's beginning, the US Marines stormed the arsenal, killed several of the rioters, and captured Brown—no arms reached slaves' hands. By other standards, Brown achieved more than he could have possibly imagined. Before the insurrection, the opposition to slavery was mostly moderate and nonviolent. It was defined not by justice but by what some call "reasonable politics": The limits were set by what white Northerners agreed to tolerate, and what they agreed to tolerate was determined by their commercial and political interests. Soon after Brown's raid, however, the abolitionist cause became radical rather than tolerant, violent rather than peaceful. The Civil War would break out less than two years after Harpers Ferry, and historians commonly agree that the incident was its "dress rehearsal." [1]

As the events at Harpers Ferry were unfolding, they were extensively covered in the nation's newspapers, as were Brown's trial and, later, execution. In pulpits, public gatherings, and editorials throughout the country—North and South—Brown was denounced as "fanatical," "maniacal," and "crazed."[2] If taking the law into his own hands earned Brown the label of a traitor, then putting the authority of universal justice above consensus—attempting to impose it on citizens—was seen as an indication of madness. At first, therefore, even abolitionists carefully distanced themselves from his act. William Lloyd Garrison, who was among the nation's best-known antislavery authors, went on the record to denounce Brown as "misguided, wild, and apparently insane."[3] Abraham Lincoln, still an aspiring presidential candidate, commented on Brown's execution: "Old John Brown has just been executed for treason against a state. We cannot object, even though he agreed with us in thinking slavery wrong. That cannot excuse violence, bloodshed, and treason."[4]

A year earlier, Lincoln had participated in a series of debates about the legitimacy of slavery with Stephen Douglas, a senator and member of the Democratic Party. Highly publicized, the debates focused on the assertion of the Declaration of Independence that "all men are created equal" and went down in history as the flamboyant media event that established American newspapers as a national power. They also ascertained Lincoln's status as an antislavery icon with presidential ambitions. His denunciation of Brown so shortly after the Lincoln-Douglas debates shows that white Americans may have been split over the question of slavery but united by a comfortable idea that preserved their national unity: The rule of law had to be upheld. Only this national unity was *their* unity just as much as this rule of law was *their* rule—a white rule of law that served to subjugate millions of women and men who had been imported like cattle, bought, sold, tortured, raped, and enslaved.

Here lies the question of radical universalism and, appearances to the contrary, it cannot be reduced to the *scope* of ethical norms. The general applicability of concepts such as "good" and "evil" is only part of the question and not the most difficult one. The deeper dispute about the Declaration of Independence was not the highly commercialized intellectual duel between Lincoln and Douglas but the unspoken one between Lincoln and Brown. The two men easily agreed in "thinking slavery wrong," as Lincoln put it. He could easily hail Thomas Jefferson for including in the Declaration "an abstract truth, valid to all men in all times." The harder challenge concerns the *authority* of this universalist proposition: Does it carry an uncompromising categorical validity, capable of overriding the authority of unjust laws and norms? Brown answered that question affirmatively in contrast to Lincoln, who, on this question, agreed with Douglas. When progressives nowadays turn their back on universalism and consider it an inherently moderate ideology that's tolerant of injustice, when they denounce it as the mask of identity politics of "white men," they oppose a form of alleged universalism that Brown, too, rejected. But whereas they assume that this is all that universalism can be, Brown defied injustice on the authority of radical universalism, an idea that he believed was biblical in origin and inscribed into politics by the Declaration of Independence. The man who W. E. B. Du Bois would call the greatest "inspiration which America owes to Africa"[5] certainly did not fight for the emancipation of slaves in the name of "identity."

The distinction between moderate and radical universalism maps well onto the familiar split in pre–Civil War America between the North's unionists and abolitionists. The unionists believed that the rule of law had to be preserved at all costs. The United States was the incarnation of democratic liberty in world history, they thought, so the unity that preserved that democracy had to be protected, even at the price of tolerating slavery. Their founding text was the United States Constitution, which, before the Civil War and the attachment of the Thirteenth Amendment, still protected slave owners' right to their property—not the inalienable rights of the humans who were that property. The abolitionists, by contrast, thought that slavery contradicted timeless metaphysical principles of justice. Since democracy was only important as a vehicle of these principles, slavery had to be ended, even at the price of jeopardizing American unity. The abolitionists' central text was not a legal document like the Constitution, which Garrison described as a "covenant with death and an agreement with hell,"[6] but the Declaration of Independence. The competing authority claims of these two documents—political versus metaphysical—defines the question of universalism: Does it culminate in the overriding authority of absolute justice and its ability to transcend human interests, laws, and constitutions; or is it reduced to the authority of man-made laws, just or unjust, to be determined by the consensus of reasonable people?

2.

For two of the country's foremost intellectuals, the answer was obvious. They sided on this question with Brown, not with Lincoln and Douglas, and they made sure to pronounce it as loudly as they could in the country's rapidly growing "public sphere." Ralph Waldo Emerson delivered a speech in Boston as Brown's trial was in full swing, hailing him as a hero, in the proper sense of the term, and therefore as anything but treasonous or mad. In an essay written after the execution, Emerson would add that Brown's heroism made his "gallows glorious like the cross."[7] Henry David Thoreau, no less of an American icon, poured his wrath upon the country's newspaper editors. The journals routinely denounce Brown as "insane," he wrote, while "the sane tyrant holds with a firmer gripe than ever his four million of slaves, and a thousand sane editors, his abettors, are saving their country."[8]

When Thoreau writes of a "tyrant," he does not refer just to the South's slaveholders. Thoreau knew well Alexis de Tocqueville's warning, in *Democracy in America*, that the country's liberty threatens to collapse into a "tyranny of the masses." In a democracy, the tendency to conform to common opinion—allowing public consensus to replace justice as the standard of judgment—can threaten freedom more powerfully than a monarch's external domination.[9] It was the captivity of minds that held slaves in its sway: The norms that allowed the toleration of slavery, even among its opponents, were based on the authority of consensus—the same authority that denounced as "fanatic" and "insane" those who act as vehicles of justice.

For Thoreau, the opportunist conformism of "newspaper editors" was proven by the fact that they cited as evidence of Brown's insanity his claim to have been "appointed." "They talk," he writes, "as if it were impossible that a man could be 'divinely appointed' in these days to do any work whatever."[10] A strange remark: Is it possible in our day to be divinely appointed? To make sense of Thoreau's comment is to take seriously an idea that was once familiar as prophecy; namely that one may obey a higher calling. But newspaper editors, so Thoreau claimed, act as prophets of conformism: "Ask the tyrant who is his most dangerous foe, the sane man or the insane?"[11]

> Republican editors, obliged to get their sentences ready for the morning edition, and accustomed to look at everything by the twilight of politics, express no admiration, nor true sorrow even, but call these men "deluded fanatics," — "mistaken men," — "insane," or "crazed." It suggests what a *sane* set of editors we are blessed with, *not* "mistaken men"; who know very well on which side their bread is buttered, at least.[12]

For Emerson, too, talk of "conformism" was a subtle reference to what Tocqueville had designated as the tyranny of the masses, and he thought it went hand in hand with the unionists' toleration of slavery. When Emerson's friend and later biographer, Oliver Wendell Holmes Sr., denounced the abolitionists as "traitors to the union," he contradicted him with rage: "As for the Union with Slavery, no manly person will suffer a day to go by without discrediting disintegrating & finally exploding it."[13] One of Emerson's favorite authors, the orator William Channing, had opposed the unionist toleration of slavery with an early Tocquevillian warning of conformism: "Our danger is, that we shall substitute the consciences of others for our own, that we shall paralyze our faculties through dependence on foreign guides, that we shall be moulded from abroad instead of determining ourselves."[14] While it is hard to prove that Channing ever read Immanuel Kant, Emerson certainly did and the continuity between his opposition to conformist tyranny and Kant's definition of Enlightenment is intriguing. A fusion of Kant and Tocqueville suggests that tolerating slavery is enabled by a breakdown of Enlightenment in the proper sense of the term—the conformist failure to "have the courage to think for one-self." Emerson's 1841 essay "Self-Reliance," now a classic, attempted to break this conformist tendency through the concept of genius: "To believe your own thought, to believe that what is true for you in your private heart is true for all men—that is genius."[15] Easy to overlook: There's hardly a man in American history who exemplified this ideal better than Brown. One reader who did not overlook this was Thoreau. That Brown had genius is just what he meant when he hailed him as appointed rather than insane.

On December 2nd, the day of Brown's execution, Victor Hugo joined his defenders. Sitting in exile in Guernsey for having denounced Napoleon III as a traitor, Hugo grasped, correctly, that the affair was not an internal American business. Given the country's role as the symbol of Enlightenment politics, the Brown affair put universal humanism on historical trial. "There is something more terrible than Cain slaying Abel," he warns. "It is

Washington slaying Spartacus!" The first, an emblem of democratic revolution; the latter, the beacon of emancipated slaves. "It seems to me," he continues, that on the day of Brown's hanging "a portion of the enlightenment of humanity would be eclipsed, that even the ideas of justice and injustice would be obscured on the day which should witness the assassination of Emancipation by Liberty."[16]

This warning deserves attention. *The enlightenment of humanity, ideas of justice and injustice, will be eclipsed once we witness the assassination of Emancipation by Liberty.* To understand this proposition, it is necessary to take seriously Hugo's comparison of Brown's execution to Cain's slaying of Abel. The parallel should be taken literally; a primordial question was at stake as Brown was brought to justice. If the original sin consisted in Adam and Eve eating the forbidden fruit from the Tree of the Knowledge of Good and Evil, which caused their expulsion from Paradise and initiated history by man's ongoing Fall, then Cain's murder of Abel marked the first act within history by the disfiguration of human brotherhood. In Genesis 4:9, when God asks Cain about his brother's whereabouts, Cain answers with a chilling rhetorical question that reverberates through the ages: "Am I my brother's keeper?" This question does not just exclude Cain from human brotherhood. The fact that it was asked, the question's sheer possibility, scars the bond of human *fraternité*.

It was the promise of the Enlightenment to heal that scar. Through universalist ideas of good and evil the Enlightenment was supposed to become an engine of progress (that is: of inverting the Fall) by restoring human brotherhood. If America as a symbol of liberty and Enlightenment undermines emancipation, then *liberté* assassinates *égalité*. It is not so much that an injustice would be done; it is that the notion of justice would be deformed. If liberty is nothing but conforming to the interests of those who are free to repeat Cain's slogan—*Am I my brother's keeper?*—then Enlightenment offers betrayal rather than hope. "What have you done?" God asks Cain in the Genesis story, "your brother's blood is shouting at me from the ground." If the American Union executed Brown because he listened to Abel's wretched voices rather than obeying common consensus, then the ideas of liberty and justice themselves would carry the mark of Cain.

3.

Sixteen years ago, when I started teaching philosophy as a young teaching assistant at Yale, I opened my Kant seminars by reading a sentence to my students and asking how many of them would endorse it: "We hold these truths to be self-evident, that all men are created equal, that they are endowed by their Creator with certain unalienable Rights, that among these are Life, Liberty and the Pursuit of Happiness,—"

The same experiment was repeated at the opening of Nietzsche lectures, too, and the results were always the same: Everyone raised their hands immediately, not to say automatically. None of the Yalies, a group of almost exclusively American "white crème," as we sometimes called them—their parents were bank CEOs, senators, editors at *The New Yorker*—had any doubts about the truths asserted in 1776 by the Founding Fathers. Or, if they did, they wouldn't let anyone notice. Of course, this was a pedagogical setup. Once the class unanimously committed to universalism, it was immediately confronted with the question of the origin of universalism, or its ground, the very same question that haunted Kant at the same time in which the Declaration was formulated. If universalist humanism has authority, why? What grounds the truths asserted in the Declaration's legendary second sentence, let alone their self-evidence? Is it science? Faith? And, if you can't answer, is your conviction any better than automatic conformism or blind religion?

It is not easy to provide these questions with a straight answer. Arguably, they have never received one that is completely satisfactory. That is why it made sense to perplex students with these allegedly self-evident truths not just before teaching Kant but also before going into Nietzsche. Sixteen years later, I still read this sentence to students, now at the New School for Social Research. But in the meantime, no one raises their hand. There is a new conformism in the air; it's the conviction that liberty *necessarily* assassinates emancipation. Students object that the Founding Fathers were slaveholders; that Kant himself was a racist; that "all men are created equal" means literally *men*, and exclusively white men. In short, that Enlightenment universalism is at best a hypocritical ideology that tolerates white supremacy, and at worst, a supremacist tool used by Europeans to colonize, expropriate, and enslave. If any of my students still support universalist values, few of them dare letting the others notice. Enlightenment has anything but overcome the mark of Cain.

It may seem too easy to import a challenge from 1776 America about the Declaration of Independence, but similar principles concern modern international constitutions and international institutions. Consider for example the first clause of German Basic Law, adopted in the shadow of the Holocaust: "Human dignity is inviolable. To respect and protect it shall be the duty of all state authority."

The same proposition about human dignity is repeated not just in German Basic Law but in the Charter of Fundamental Rights of the European Union. The United Nations Universal Declaration of Human Rights, adopted on December 10, 1948, similarly appeals to human dignity in its first clause: "All human beings are born free and equal in dignity and rights." And the preamble opens by stating its "Faith in the fundamental human rights [and] in the dignity and worth of the human person."

The attachment to the idea that human dignity is inviolable in postwar European and international institutions is the counterpart of the notion that humans self-evidently have inalienable rights. It is but the modern expression of the return to Enlightenment universalism. Here are the questions, then: Is the principle of human dignity, tied as it is to Enlightenment universalism, actually an expression of the white West's colonialism and racism? Should we defend the idea of human dignity or "decolonize" such documents as the United Nations Universal Declaration of Human Rights from it? Is German Basic Law, asserting human dignity as *unantastbar*, the legal answer to past crimes, or, in a deep sense, its cause? Not less important, if we support such notions, if we genuinely support the idea of dignity, what is its ground?

According to the preamble of the Declaration of Independence, our rights as humans were given to us by our "Creator"—earlier in the text, the Founding Fathers appeal also to the "station" given to us by "Nature's God"—but, from the perspective of contemporary political theory, grounding universalism in God is obviously futile.

The most familiar move has been to replace God with nature. On this view, human beings have inalienable *natural* rights: By nature, humans have a right to their bodies. By nature, we have the freedom of speech. This appeal to nature rather than God may sound more convincing to modern ears but it shouldn't, and the reason is not far to seek. Within a premodern, broadly Aristotelian metaphysics, it might make sense to appeal to nature in order to ground rights and norms. John Locke, the father of modern liberalism, still accepted such a metaphysics, and there is no doubt that Jefferson, Washington, Adams, Madison et al. viewed the Declaration of Independence as an expression of his *Second Treatise of Government*.[17] If one follows them in thinking that nature proceeds according to some telos, or divine intention, which is in turn considered good, then one can also adduce nature as a source of universal value. The inherent worth of human beings can be then derived from the "station" that they occupy in a natural order that is morally organized: Violating their rights is going against nature's moral purpose; it is wrong as an objective fact. Once a teleological concept of nature is abandoned, however, and blind mechanism takes over as the Enlightenment's only valid description of nature, the idea of natural rights becomes as empty as the idea that humans received their rights from God.[18]

Another way to understand this predicament is to notice that universalist justice cannot be, strictly speaking, universal. Since universalism is a thesis about value, it actually depends on the existence of hierarchies and exclusions. To meaningfully say that "everybody" is equal, one must be prepared to say that everybody who falls within a certain category (say, humans) has more rights than whoever or whatever falls outside that category (donkeys, stones). Stating that everything is equal is stating that nothing has value at all: This is exactly where modern science leaves ethics and politics. On November 24, 1859, in the short interim between Brown's conviction and his execution, Charles Darwin's *On the Origin of Species* was published, revolutionizing the perception of humans almost overnight. For the first time, science reduced human beings to nature's blind evolution, a development whose consequences Nietzsche would articulate almost immediately in the statement: "Life is essentially something amoral."[19] Once not even humans can be viewed as occupying a unique "station" within nature, the set of equals is extended to everything. In our "remote corner of the universe," as Nietzsche puts it, on our forsaken star on which "clever animals invented knowledge," not just all humans are equal but all animals, vegetables, and stones.[20] Talk of inalienable natural rights thus becomes either deliberately fictional—at best, a noble lie—or meaningless. Blind evolution endows clever beasts with all sorts of desires, powers, and urges, not by natural rights.

In other words, there is a sense in which a premodern, metaphysical understanding of the world is a necessary condition of modern liberalism. Atheist and post-metaphysical liberals, if they purport to endorse universalism at all, do not just endorse it without sufficient rational foundations; they make use of a tradition that they repudiate.[21] In this view, it is not surprising that their universalism tends to hypocrisy, a politics that's only couched in a language of equality—or human dignity as an absolute, "inviolable" norm—but is motivated at best by hegemonic identity and at worst by the interests of the powerful. Jürgen Habermas, a longtime post-metaphysical thinker who takes pride in turning a "deaf ear" to religion, drew the ire of fellow secularists when he claimed, in his 2008 "post-secular" Yale Lectures, that religion should not be merely tolerated by modern liberal thinkers but *listened to*.[22] Some religious content "eludes" the explanatory force of philosophical language, he frankly admitted, and in this sense may "resist translation."[23] But what if what resists translation is what Enlightenment modernity used to take pride in; what if what eludes translation is the idea of universalism itself?

If neither God nor nature can help us take the commitment to human dignity as inviolable or human rights as inalienable, what are the other options? There are still two, interrelated alternatives to consider, namely appealing to history. Or, similarly, to grounding our commitments in the decision of a political community to constitute itself according to some idea—by means of becoming conscious of its own historical circumstances.

It is thus tempting to assume in post-metaphysical circles that a principle like the one that's articulated in the first clause of German Basic Law, or the United Nations Universal Declaration of Human Rights, could be *grounded* in the decision of a people —say, the Germans, in view of past horrors and crimes—to bind itself to the idea that human dignity is "inviolable." Similarly, the emphasis in "We hold these truths to be self-evident" is not on the truths and their self-evidence—which was left ungrounded— but on "we": *We* hold these truths to be self-evident; these truths matter because this is who *we* are.

But this prevalent answer is, in fact, begging the question—in both theory and practice. The claim that human dignity obtains, say, for the German people given German history, amounts to admitting that it needn't apply to others. Other nations, given their own particular past, may not constitute themselves by the obligation to respect human dignity. For example, Jews, given *their* history, may be inclined to say that in the interest of their self-defense they are entitled to violate this principle—avoid it in war, and avoid it in constitutions that begin with an unqualified commitment to human dignity that may question the idea of Jewish sovereignty. How do Germans, if they ground their own commitment to dignity in history, relate to such a claim?

46

And how do they do that all the more given that similar claims could be raised, and obviously are being raised, by yet others—say, the Palestinians? For the time being this question is raised not to debate a painful political question that has arguably failed a whole post-war German tradition of universalism and international law, but to notice the theoretical point: Once one recognizes *externally* that others may have the right to violate human dignity, one also recognizes something *internally*, and that is that one cannot claim human dignity as inviolable anymore, for you have recognized, given history, your duty to respect that others may be entitled to violate it. Insofar as this principle is grounded in history, then history also threatens to mark the scope of the commitment. It is no longer universal. In fact, the issue isn't just the commitment's scope, it is the very meaning of the humanistic propositions in question. If the principle of human dignity is grounded in the decision of a people to accept it, then that's actually the very explanation why that principle is *not* inviolable or inalienable. Whatever depends on the will of anyone—God, a king, the people—is violable. It is very nice that, say, the German people have decided to submit to the idea of human dignity. As we know, they can also decide otherwise. And not just they.

To return to Habermas's post-secular statement, then, what if what resists translation into modernity is actually what modernity has usually taken pride in; what if what eludes translation from metaphysical and religious forms of thought is the idea of universalism itself?

Needless to say, if this question is raised to convince secular universalists to accept faith, it is useless. They reject the belief in God or teleology not merely because they oppose their religiosity. Nor do they oppose them because they recognize in religion an illiberal or a nondemocratic potential. Such premodern concepts of nature are rejected because they are contradicted by science: Accepting God or teleology as the origin of value is rightly deemed irrational. This, in turn, aggravates their—I should say, our—predicament. Far from being self-evident, universalist propositions seem from the perspective of reason indistinguishable from silence.

4.

Another word for this silence is nihilism. The term is often associated with Nietzsche, but it dates back a hundred years earlier, to the final days of the Enlightenment. It was coined by Friedrich Heinrich Jacobi, who argued that Enlightenment philosophy necessarily leads to the overriding naturalism of Spinoza's *Ethics*.[24] Up until recently, it was common to assume that Spinoza's philosophy was forgotten as Enlightenment thinking unfolded.

We now know that even if philosophers preferred engaging with Spinoza between the lines, the impact of his writings (the *Ethics* was "forged in Hell by a renegade Jew and the Devil," as one particularly ungenerous critic put it[25]) was ubiquitous. Spinoza's unrelenting rationalism, reducing God to blind nature and rejecting all teleological explanations as irrational, was among the most powerful engines of the radical Enlightenment all along.[26]

The significance of this oft-overlooked historical detail cannot be overstated. It shows that modernity did not need Darwin's 1859 *On the Origin of Species* to reduce the station of humanity in creation to the blind abyss of natural mechanism. Through Spinoza, Enlightenment philosophy understood this nihilist reduction two hundred years before science did; and, through Spinoza, it drew ethical conclusions much like Nietzsche would. According to Spinoza's *Ethics*, it is a self-evident truth, known with the certainty of a geometrical demonstration , that everything in nature proceeds by blind, logical necessity. An independent and universal measure of justice can therefore direct human thinking in Spinoza's *sub specie aeternitatis* just as little as it can in Nietzsche's out-of-the-way corner of the universe. In fact, with a deliberate nod to the story of Adam and Eve, Spinoza attempts to undo good and evil as irrational concepts that promote violence similarly to intolerant religion. The ethics of the *Ethics* culminates in the proposition that we never "will" or "desire anything because we judge it to be good"—we only judge a thing to be good "because we . . . desire it."[27] Since desire is forever *our* desire, that notion produces no universal moral categories, hence the doctrine that reason entails interests rather than duties, that the good or the just are indistinguishable from the powerful.

In this view, the *Ethics* could just as well have been titled *Beyond Good and Evil*. It introduces not merely an early articulation of the "inversion of all values," but also of the idea that moral universalism is slave morality. "If men were born free," Spinoza writes, "they would form no concept of good and evil so long as they remained free."[28] Such free men are "rational," whereas irrational men, following the illusion of objective and absolute moral norms, are "slaves." If any biblical narrative conveyed for Spinoza a deep truth, it wasn't the moral universalism that was taught by the prophets but the doctrine that's conveyed "from the whirlwind" as God repudiated Job's cry for justice: "Who is this that darkens counsel without knowledge? . . . Where were you when I laid the foundations of the earth?"[29] Demanding justice is dismissed in God's words quite literally as an ignorant lack of enlightenment. Subjecting reality to a universal standard of justice—and, if universal, then one by which God also ought to be judged—is mocked as an anthropomorphic fallacy. To know God is to know that nature just *is*. Spinoza's deconstruction rather than a translation of the prophet's revolutionary call for justice was the reason why not just seventeenth-century religious author-ities like the Amsterdam Portuguese Synagogue but also a liberal Jewish thinker like Hermann Cohen condemned Spinoza in the harshest terms. He found in Spinoza's philosophy a "humanly inconceivable betrayal."[30] A biblical figure like Brown, "appointed" to emancipate slaves in the name of eternal justice, would have been to both Spinoza and Nietzsche a fanatic prophet of slave morality. It is not surprising that Nietzsche found in the Jew from Amsterdam a kindred spirit. The differences between their philosophies, he observes, are only due to differences of "time, culture and science":

> I have a *precursor*, and what a precursor! ... in five main points of his doctrine I recognize myself ... he denies the freedom of the will, teleology, the moral world order, the unegoistic, and evil. ... *In summa*: my lonesomeness, which, as on very high mountains, often made it hard for me to breathe and made my blood rush out, is now at least a twosomeness. Strange.[31]

Far from a "twosomeness," however, the naturalist position sketched by Nietzsche is the inheritance of Enlightenment moder-nity. And in this continuity between Spinoza's naturalism and Nietzsche's Darwinism, a common mistake stands to be corrected: Universalism is not the inheritance of Enlightenment thinking.

It is Enlightenment rationalism—not the anti-rationalism of the anti-Enlightenment or the postmodernism that followed it—that challenges universalism most vehemently. That's also the reason for which it bears the mark of Cain: If Enlightenment philosophy promoted an ideology of interest and power, if it enabled and sponsored European enslavers and colonialists, in short, if the Enlightenment assassinated emancipation, it was not because it guarded (much less invented) universalism but because it undermined it.

5.

That's the crisis to which Kant's philosophical revolution was designed to respond. If anti-universalist nihilism is the consequence of Enlightenment rationalism, Kant's *Critique of Pure Reason* could just as well have been called *Critique of Enlightenment*. His attempt to salvage universalism from the Enlightenment proceeds in two main stages, corresponding to Kant's assertion, in the opening of the *Critique*, "I found it necessary to deny knowledge, in order to make room for faith."[32] This is one of the best-known sentences in Kant's *Werke*, but insisting as it does on faith as opposed to knowledge it tends to embarrass modern readers. What does it mean?

First, the denial of knowledge: Kant found it necessary to limit the scope of Enlightenment naturalism because he saw that it led to Spinozist nihilism, in which a "human being would be a marionette or an automaton."[33] In such an anti-humanist outlook, the freedom to follow moral precepts "would be mere delusion."[34] Enlightenment philosophers, Kant complains, have "shown more shrewdness than sincerity in keeping this difficult point out of sight as much as possible, in the hope that if they said nothing about it no one would be likely to think of it."[35] It was necessary to clip the wings of Enlightenment rationalism to prevent it from turning into a form of positivist anti-humanism. Without this denial of knowledge, "nothing remains but Spinozism."[36]

Kant's criticism of reason is best understood by comparison to the work of Spinoza himself. In the *Theological-Political Treatise*, Spinoza asks to make room for Enlightenment rationalism by inaugurating the method of biblical criticism: He systematically questions the authority of faith by subjecting the alleged truth of biblical revelation to rational inquiry. The Bible was to be studied as any other text, created by the individual authors who wrote it, not as an expression of prophetic authority. Kant agreed on this point with Spinoza, of course, but he thought that what Spinoza did to biblical narrative had to be done to reason as well: Its authority had to be questioned. Otherwise, rationalism would itself become a form of despotic authority that undermines

Enlightenment. In this sense, *Critique of Pure Reason* functions as a *Theological-Political Treatise*. It offers not biblical criticism but reason criticism—preventing a mechanist religion of reason. "Criticism alone," Kant writes, "can sever the root [*Wurzel*] of *materialism, fatalism, atheism, free-thinking, fanaticism* [*Schwärmerei*], and *superstition*" which threaten to follow from Enlightenment rationalism and affect "the public, not just learned," undermining its own political aspirations.[37]

The book culminates in Kant's claim that mechanistic naturalism cannot provide a coherent description of reality as a whole: Once positivist naturalism is taken for a thoroughgoing description of everything, it collapses into "darkness and contradictions,"[38] that is, the opposite of Enlightenment. Among other things, because the authority of science depends on the authority of thinking, a scientific reduction of thinking to blind mechanistic processes undermines the authority of science itself. It reduces knowledge to myth or, as Nietzsche would later derive from Darwin, to "a mobile army of metaphors," where truth is an illusion that depends on our "forgetting" that illusion is all that it is.[39] The authority of Enlightenment science, therefore, can only be preserved by critically exposing its necessary limits, showing that human thinking remains outside its jurisdiction. A hundred years before Darwin, Kant knew well why science cannot and ought not make human thinking an object of knowledge.

This circumscription of knowledge in turn made "room for faith." It is tempting to suspect that "faith" in this sentence stands for a moderate move to censor the radical potential of secular modernity, and no doubt this is also how readers have interpreted that sentence for generations.[40] This temptation ought to be resisted. Faith in Kant is anything but a form of conservative or obedient submission; on the contrary, it emerges as the antidote against any form of illegitimate authority or power. Kant could have opened the *Critique* announcing that he "had to deny knowledge" in order to "make room for *thinking*"—and thinking in the most potent sense of the term: of attaining truth beyond factual knowledge; of creating novel ideas beyond conformism; of recognizing the duty to justice beyond interests and consensus; of radical hope beyond resignation to the status quo. In Kant, no foreign authority limits thinking, be it religion, science, the state, or, as we shall see, God. And the capacity to think freely—to think for oneself—replaces God or nature as the ground of radical universalism.

To understand Kant's maneuver, it is useful to focus on his account of "immaturity" in "What Is Enlightenment?" The essay opens with this well-known passage,

Enlightenment is mankind's exit from its self-incurred immaturity. Immaturity is the inability to make use of one's own understanding without the guidance of another. *Self-incurred* is this inability if its cause lies not in the lack of understanding but rather in the lack of the resolution and the courage to use it without guidance of another. *Sapere aude!* Have the courage to use your *own* understanding! is thus the motto of enlightenment.[41]

The idea that immaturity is "self-incurred" is the axis on which Kant's revolution takes place. In animals, maturity is a natural given. A bird will inevitably learn to fly, a cheetah will develop speed, and so would all animals mature: Unless impeded by external misfortunes, they naturally become full-fledged representatives of their species. In humans, the meaning of maturity is different. It is inseparable from taking responsibility, an achievement that depends on the ability to think independently and is anything but ensured.[42] Healthy grown-ups can and do fail to think freely as adults. Societies can be ones that foster or impede *Selbstdenken*. Bringing one's human capacity to fruition is not a consequence that happens to humans by nature, it is their *Aufgabe* as individuals and groups.

By centralizing the concept of maturity in the 1784 essay, then, Kant made the question "What is a human being?" key to answering the question "What is Enlightenment?" And by pointing out that human maturity depends on responsibility, he didn't quite tell us what humans are but mostly what they aren't: They aren't beings of nature. Humanity cannot be conceived as a biological species any more than it can as a zoological, historical, anthropological, or sociological concept. Neither would Darwinian science reduce humanity to blind evolution—to think that it can is to misunderstand the concept as biological in the first place. Humanity can only be a moral concept.

To say that humanity can only be a moral concept is to insist that it depends on one characteristic only: freedom. Whereas animal species are defined by biological facts about their body, whereas what mature animals are supposed to do can be known by empirically studying what they are doing, humans are defined by more than the concrete facts that define their identity and actions. They are free because reasons and justifications can determine their behavior, not just causes. Moral precept can motivate them, not just interest. Their humanity consists in the fact that, in contrast to natural species, *who* they are cannot be reduced to *what* they are. It depends not on what they do or on how they live but on their being open to the call of what they *ought* to be doing.

This Kantian distinction between "is" and "ought" is familiar enough but often gets misunderstood. Kant's friends have often contributed to its misunderstanding, too, because it has been convenient to sell his thinking by downplaying the robust metaphysics that lie at its heart. It is only the abstract idea of humanity as independent from nature that gives humans the respect that they command. By contrast to natural beings that belong to an aimless nature, humans are free to set moral ends. Therefore, they themselves ought to be categorically treated as ends, never as mere means. They don't just have value—things can acquire value by being used. Rather, they have a dignity that's "exalted above all values," that is, absolute. As Kant explains in *Groundwork of the Metaphysics of Morals*:

> Everything has either a *price* or a *dignity*. What has a price can be replaced by something else as its *equivalent*; what on the other hand is raised above all price and therefore admits of no equivalent . . . has not merely a relative worth, that is, a price, but an inner worth, that is, *dignity*.
>
> Now, morality is the condition under which alone a rational being can be an end in itself, since only through this is it possible to be [free]. . . . Hence morality, and humanity insofar as it is capable of morality, is that which alone has dignity.[43]

Slavery is the paradigmatic violation of this absolute principle because it is premised on the systematic reduction of humans to mere means. Tolerating this institution in the name of any circumstance or value (say, prosperity, order, peace, or democratic consensus) doesn't just normalize an injustice; it deforms the ground of justice. No constitution, law, or political order that protects slavery can have legitimate authority because it mutilates the foundation of all values and thereby the basis of any authority at all. It isn't surprising, therefore, that in the paragraph above Kant insinuates a repudiation of slavery—humans can have no "price"—as a direct corollary of the categorical imperative.

Once Kant's argument is understood, it shows that dignity, abstraction, universalism, and authority are inseparable. Dignity depends on freedom, which is the capacity not to be determined by concrete facts. Therefore, it can only be abstract. Since it is abstract, it is universal in scope, applying to all. And for the same reason, it is also categorical, that is, universal in authority: No circumstance or consideration can ever interfere or undermine it. Kant's grounding of universalism in the abstract concept of humanity recovers the duty to a higher principle of justice. Universal norms are about humans but transcend any human authority.

Which, in turn, is the basis of the faith for which Kant's denial of knowledge had made room. It expresses his Copernican Revolution as a revolution in the proper sense of the term, because it overthrows absolute authority and replaces it with another: We do not accept the authority of justice because God commands it; rather, we have faith because, facing the demand of justice, we recognize an unconditional authority that could not have been man-made.[44] For Kant, it is Job's demand of justice—his condemnation of God as unjust—not God's answer to that charge from the whirlwind, that reveals the deep insight of biblical faith and calls for philosophical translation. Job "proved that he did not found his morality on faith," he writes, "but his faith on morality."[45] It is remarkable that God, too, confirms that Job "spoke the truth" about him.[46]

In fact, biblical narrative expresses the meaning of Kant's ethics-based faith even more boldly in Abraham's figure. Having learned that God is about to destroy the cities of Sodom and Gomorrah and all their inhabitants, he approaches God in protest: "Will you also destroy the righteous with the wicked? ... Far be it from you to do such a thing, to slay the righteous with the wicked, so that the righteous would be as the wicked. Far be it from you. Shall not the judge of all the earth do what is just?"[47] In this speech, Abraham, fully conscious of his finite human condition ("I am but dust and ashes," he'll say in the next sentence) is appointed—that is, he acts as a prophet—but he isn't divinely appointed in any familiar sense of the term. Abraham embodies a peculiar form of prophecy because it is at once a more radical expression of that term and more modern: Since justice is universal, it stands not just above the earthly authority of kings, as familiar from other prophets, but also above the authority of the one true deity.

The main innovation of biblical monotheism, in this view, is not merely the introduction of an intolerant Mosaic distinction, as Jan Assmann argues in continuity with Freud (and with Nietzsche and Spinoza)—the idea that this God is true and others aren't. It is rather the discovery of an Abrahamic view: This justice is true and all others aren't, therefore, it stands also above the authority of the only true deity. In fact, in this moral speech against God's injustice, Abraham's monotheism emerges as the exact opposite of Moses's, who brings to the people God's imposed, written, allegedly universal law from Mount Sinai. Moses thus expresses the idea that universalist ethics are based on the authority of the one deity. Abraham's point is that universalist ethics can only stand above the deity. Kant most likely did not know that Job's faith, his call for justice, was modeled after Abraham's. When he protests injustice, he asks, "Who has resisted Him and succeeded?"[48] "He destroys both the righteous and the wicked (צדיק ורשע) . . . he mocks at the calamity of the innocent. Who would tell him, what are you doing? (מה תעשה?)"[49] This rhetorical question bears an implicit but unmistakable reference to a text in which it had received an answer. Abraham resisted God and told him exactly that—"far be it from you to do such a thing (מעשות כדבר הזה)" and succeeded in preventing him from destroying "the righteous and the wicked (צדיק ורשע)."[50] There, his ability to contradict God's authority on the basis of universal justice was in turn the reason for which Abraham becomes the father of all nations. God had in the first place shared with Abraham his intention to destroy the city of Sodom, knowing that "all the nations of the earth shall be blessed in him. They may keep the way of the Eternal, to do righteousness and justice."[51] Universal scope and universal authority go hand in hand.

If despite this speech Kant highlighted Job rather than Abraham as his model of faith, this is because Abraham is mostly remembered not for this remarkably Kantian scene in Sodom but for the Binding of Isaac.[52] There, God tests Abraham and monotheism by commanding that the father sacrifice his "only beloved son," and Abraham allegedly withstands the trial by complying. His model of monotheistic faith is thus famous for presenting the violently opposite one of Kant's—a model in which, as Kierkegaard would put it, both justice and indeed the "universal" are overcome. I return to the Binding of Isaac in chapter 3. For now, suffice it to notice that on the strength of his Copernican Revolution, Kant becomes the first thinker in history to explicitly denounce Abraham's obedience, and that this denunciation could be derived from the same faith that Abraham himself exemplified in Sodom and that Job repeats. "Abraham," Kant says, "should have replied to this supposedly divine voice: 'That I ought not to kill my son is quite certain. But that you, this apparition, are God—of that I am not certain, and never can be, not even if this voice rings down to me from (visible) heaven.'"[53]

One reader who grasped the political significance of this position was Heinrich Heine. Dubbing Kant the "*alles zermalmender*," he comments that *Critique of Pure Reason* was the "sword" with which God's authority was toppled: Robespierre may have managed to chop a king's head off; Kant toppled not a head but a whole way of thinking. Properly understood, this revolution "far surpassed Maximilien Robespierre in terrorism."[54]

If we return to the Declaration of Independence, this comment appears accurate. Insofar as its self-evident truths are interpreted as the Lockean propositions that Jefferson et al. intended them to be, it remains idle. But as Kant once argued, we can "understand [an author] better than he has understood himself,"[55] and the Declaration is a striking case in point. Interpreted as a Kantian document, its universalism regains its original revolutionary significance: Since the truths it pronounces are absolute, they stand above any human agreement or government, despotic or democratic.

That the document's original significance lies here becomes clear from a careful look at the preamble's second sentence. It is much longer than the part that's commonly remembered by heart:

> We hold these truths to be self-evident, that all MEN are created
> equal, that they are endowed by their Creator with certain

unalienable Rights, that among these are Life, Liberty and the pursuit of Happiness,— That to secure these rights, Governments are instituted among Men, deriving their just powers from the consent of the governed,— That whenever any Form of Government becomes destructive of these ends, it is the Right of the People to alter or to abolish it, and to institute new Government, laying its foundation on such principles and organizing its powers in such form, as to them shall seem most likely to effect their Safety and Happiness.

The complete sentence strongly suggests the structure of an argument, a syllogism, of which the first famous part is only the premise.[56] The parts of the syllogism are marked by semicolons:

a. All MEN are created equal;
b. Governments are created to secure their equal rights; therefore,
c. When any government undermines these rights, the right to abolish the law and revolt follow.

The argument is logically valid, that is, the conclusion—the right of revolution—follows from the premises. Its soundness depends on the strength of the main premise, and that premise is radical universalism itself: the idea that final authority lies with truth. If this truth is denied or depends on the authority of human agreement, the right of revolution would not follow. For that reason, the premise has to assert an absolute truth about humans —not about citizens, not about "the people." Here is a subtle but important point: The *meaning* of the claim that all men are created equal cannot be understood without the end of the sentence, which derives the right of revolution from a self-evident truth. The universal scope and authority of this truth must be taken literally.

Cynics may dismiss this Kantian vindication of the Declaration by pointing out that Jefferson himself was a Southern slaveowner, and that his talk of "MEN" by all means refers to concrete facts about them—the reference is exclusively to white males. This error is widespread nowadays and ought to be corrected; its roots are deeper and more pernicious than usually perceived. The first to come up with this absurdity seems to have been Chief Justice Roger Taney, in his Dred Scott decision of 1857, which determined that the US Constitution does not protect Black citizens, whether free or enslaved. Stephen Douglas reiterated the same view in his debates with Lincoln. The latter repeatedly complained that, before Dred Scott, there had never been a man "in the whole world who said that the Declaration of Independence did not include negroes in the term 'all men'" but, after the decision, "it has become the catchword of the entire [Democratic] party."[57] Lincoln did not tire of pointing out that before the decision, not even the worst supremacist denied the inclusion of Blacks in "all MEN." Just the contrary, recognizing that it does, they turned vehemently against the Declaration of Independence.[58] John Calhoun, the chief ideologue of the South, dubbed the Declaration's self-evident "axiom" as the "most false and dangerous of all political errors."[59] Following his cue, John Pettit, a Democratic representative, made a name for himself by coining the catchphrase that the Declaration was nothing but "a self-evident lie."[60] Clearly, these supremacists recognized the threat that truth posed to their politics. It is a grave error for today's progressives to dismiss this truth and the document that asserts it with Taney, Douglas, Calhoun, and Pettit rather than rehabilitate it with Lincoln or Brown. For what it's worth, there is no doubt that Jefferson, despite owning slaves, did include Black people in the proposition. This is clear from a reading of the original draft, which includes this paragraph:

[King George III] has waged cruel war against human nature itself, violating its most sacred rights of life & liberty in the persons of a distant people who never offended him, captivating & carrying them into slavery in another hemisphere, or to incur miserable death in their transportation thither. This piratical warfare, the opprobrium of infidel powers, is the warfare of the

> Christian king of Great Britain, determined to keep open a market where MEN should be bought & sold.[61]

This part was eventually elided by Congress but referring to slave markets as places where "MEN" are being sold it shows that "MEN" in the text means Blacks just as much as white property owners. Since in said slave markets women and children were also sold, it is hard to escape the conclusion that "MEN" means just what we normally mean by the concept: humans.

And then of course one must also address Kant's racist comments. He wrote, for example, that humans achieve their "greatest perfection" in whites, while "yellow Indians" have a "meager talent...negroes are far below them, and at the lowest point are a part of the American people."[62] That Kant held such opinions cannot and ought not be denied, and he even included them in his "scientific" writings on anthropology. Nevertheless, the currently common reaction to these quotes is not to hold Kant the man accountable for failing to live up to his own ideals; it is rather to use his failings to delegitimize the ideals themselves. The underlying charge is not that Kant held discriminatory views, which he obviously did, but that treating humanity as a universal moral abstraction is somehow the reason for this discrimination. In what is probably the defining article on the topic in the United States, the late Charles Mills goes so far as to argue that Kant's humanist abstraction is responsible for the "division between the *Herrenvolk* and *Untermenschen*, persons and subpersons, upon which Nazi history would later draw."[63] Arguments of this sort are accepted with enthusiasm on campuses and create a culture in which radical humanism isn't just criticized but canceled.

Paradoxically, the power of Kant's abstract concept of humanity is all the clearer in light of his ugly comments about Asians, Black people, and Native Americans. Because freedom is independent from anthropological and cultural features just as much as it is from biology, so is human dignity. No matter what this Prussian philosophy professor thought two hundred years ago about Blacks, he still had no doubt that "There can be nothing more horrendous than that the action of a human being shall stand under the will of another. Hence no antipathy can be more natural than that which a human being has toward slavery."[64] In other words, taking Kant's two-hundred-year-old anthropology as somehow relevant to Kantian ethics can only be accomplished by a misunderstanding, deliberate or not, of his main achievement: excluding by a metaphysical abstraction all facts—anthropological, historical, sociological, psychological, biological—from consideration of human dignity. "The class of whites cannot be separated as a special kind from that of blacks in Human Kind; and there are no different kinds of humans at all."[65]

In line with this claim, Kant criticized, at least late in his career, not just slavery but colonialist exploitation of "primitive" societies in Africa, advocating for democratic institutions in all of them.[66] And even if he called Native American societies "savage," he supported signing contracts with them, an act that for Kant strictly assumes humanity and freedom on both sides.[67] It is one thing to be morally scandalized by two-hundred-year-old talk of "primitive" and "savage" societies, and quite another to use these words to show that abstract universalism informs racism. The truth is exactly the opposite: Without the abstract idea of humanity, it is unclear what's wrong with racism in the first place. Once concrete facts about humans replace Kant's abstraction, the delicate ground of absolute dignity is compromised. All laws become man-made, open to the negotiation of interests and power. One opens the door not just to the toleration of slavery but to legitimizing it: If humans are conceived concretely, it is hard to see why they cannot be treated as objects—means rather than ends. Kant, a Prussian philosophy professor, does not inflate adjectives when he argues that no crime is more *horrendous* than slavery. He understands it as a primordial offense against the categorical imperative; understands that tolerating it, as Hugo would later write, is not accepting an injustice but assassinating the very idea of justice. Call Kant a racist: When Heine said his revolutionary terrorism surpassed Robespierre's, that's because like Emerson, Thoreau, and Hugo, he would have supported Brown.

6.

On April 10, 1963, an Alabama city court issued a ban against Black activists' intention to march in Birmingham against segregation. Martin Luther King Jr., who had just pledged to bring the civil rights campaign to "the most thoroughly segregated city" in America,[68] announced that he would defy the court's ruling, marched, and was incarcerated. As King was sitting in solitary confinement, a group of white clergymen, seven pastors and one rabbi, challenged his methods in an open letter, titled "A Call for Unity."[69] Circulated broadly, it is safe to assume that this call resonated with progressive liberals, also in the North. The clergymen made it clear that they sympathized with the goals of the Civil Rights Movement but opposed King's methods. Having previously published a similar pamphlet on civil rights activism titled "An Appeal for Law and Order and Common Sense," they now called upon King to remain reasonable.[70] He was agitating in Alabama as an "outsider," they charged, disrupting peace in the name of an "impatient," "unwise," and "untimely" justice—they might have said "abstract" and "metaphysical." Worst of all, he was disobeying the law and the courts.[71]

King's response is now an American classic. He points out that he never bothers answering criticisms but addresses this one, recognizing that it is coming from people of "good will."[72] To the clergymen's claim that he agitates in Alabama as an "outsider," he answered that "injustice anywhere is a threat to justice everywhere."[73] To their claim that he was being "impatient" and "untimely," he replied that these "white moderates" lack the appropriate experience. In today's terms, he sends them to check their privilege: "We have waited for more than 340 years for our constitutional and God-given rights," he says. "Perhaps it is easy for those who have never felt the stinging darts of segregation to say, 'Wait.'" But for all those who have watched "vicious mobs" lynch their "mothers and fathers," or hateful police officers "curse, kick and even kill … black brothers and sisters" will understand why it's difficult to wait. "There comes a time when the cup of endurance runs over, and men are no longer willing to be plunged into the abyss of despair."[74] Against the "ill will" of its enemies, says King, the Civil Rights Movement will prevail; it is the hypocritical "good will" of moderates that poses the real threat. The great "stumbling block in [the Negro's] stride toward freedom is not the White Citizen's Councilor or the Ku Klux Klanner, but the white moderate who is more devoted to order than to justice."[75] Among other things, this illuminates in painful irony King's reasons for answering the clergymen: He said that he answers them because he recognizes their "good will"; it now turns out that he does so because he considers the goodwill of moderates more pernicious than the ill will of racists. Like Thoreau, whom King read carefully, he understands that conformism to law can become the greatest enemy of justice.

But if sixty years after King's "Letter from Birmingham Jail" can be read in schools on Martin Luther King Day and greeted by consensus, often by the same type of moderates who would have, at the time, repudiated him, it's because the text's deeper meanings are conveniently overlooked. King's letter remains completely misunderstood before one comes to terms with his answer to the clergymen's charge that he violates the rule of law:

> Since we so diligently urge people to obey the Supreme Court's decision of 1954 outlawing segregation in the public schools, at first glance it may seem rather paradoxical for us consciously to break laws. One may well ask: "How can you advocate breaking some laws and obeying others?" The answer lies in the fact that there are two types of laws: just and unjust. I would be the first to advocate obeying just laws. One has not only a legal but a moral responsibility to obey just laws. Conversely, one has a moral responsibility to disobey unjust laws. I would agree with St. Augustine that "an unjust law is no law at all."[76]

If this proposition is taken seriously, it contradicts the liberal idea that democratic procedures bestow legitimate authority. It subjects law not just to constitutions but to justice, understood metaphysically. Even not-so-moderate thinkers on the far margins of a remotely liberal left would hesitate before endorsing Augustine's statement. King meant that endorsement seriously, indeed it was the heart of his message. As he went on to explain, "How does one determine whether a law is just or unjust? A just law is a man-made code that squares with the moral law or the law of God. An unjust law is a code that is out of harmony with the moral law. To put it in the terms of St. Thomas Aquinas: An unjust law is a human law that is not rooted in eternal law and natural law."[77] The answer to pernicious moderation is not post-Enlightenment ideology but universalism taken as a serious doctrine. And the problem with King's position is not that such universalism isn't taken seriously enough; it is that it has become easy to take it so unseriously that many moderates can commit to the same "moral law" as an empty shell and then go on with the comfortable consensus. Short of reclaiming an "eternal" or "natural" law, the Birmingham letter remains as empty as the Declaration of Independence. Indeed, the Declaration is at the heart of King's "extremist" alternative to pernicious moderation: "Was not Thomas Jefferson an extremist? 'We hold these truths to be self-evident, that all men are created equal.' The question is not whether we will be extremist, but what kind of extremists we will be. Will we be extremists for hate, or will we be extremists for love? Will we be extremists for the preservation of injustice, or will we be extremists for the cause of justice?"[78]

Progressive activists and commentators would be tempted to interpret this reference to Jefferson as naïve. But the leader of the Civil Rights Movement knew well that Jefferson held slaves. What's more, King had just condemned the goodwill of moderates as more dangerous to justice than the Ku Klux Klan: He understands as well as anyone that hypocritical universalism bears the mark of Cain and would assassinate emancipation. Come to think of it, this is just the argument of his Birmingham letter. But King does not for all that dismiss the Declaration as a moderate text. Following the abolitionist tradition, he enlists it as the document that defies the authority of the Supreme Court and man-made law in the name of "eternal" justice. He is committed to the proposition that all men are created equal, not to the law of "the people."

The force of this commitment is the clearest in King's response to the Vietnam War. When the Birmingham letter was written, Vietnam was already raging, operating increasingly as a catalyst of Black emancipation. The war shattered social barriers, created new bonds between white and Black soldiers, and propelled states to recognize their obligation toward Black veterans. It also encouraged President Lyndon Baines Johnson, who was digging up support for the war in all corners, to promote and sign into law civil rights bills that could increase his backing among Black voters. Nevertheless, facing heavy pressures from fellow civil rights leaders, King took a vocal stand against his country's war policy. Breaking the "betrayal of his own silence," as he later put it, he opened his anti-war sermon, "Transformed Non-Conformist," with a quote of Paul from Romans 12:2: "And be not conformed to this world: but be ye transformed by the renewing of your mind." The meaning of resisting "conformism" receives concrete interpretation in a later speech:

As I have called for radical departures from the destruction of Vietnam, many persons have questioned me about the wisdom of my path. At the heart of their concerns this query has often loomed large and loud: Why are *you* speaking about the war, Dr. King? Why are *you* joining the voices of dissent? Peace and civil rights don't mix, they say. Aren't you hurting the cause of your people, they ask? And when I hear them, though I often understand the source of their concern, I am nevertheless greatly saddened, for such questions mean that the inquirers have not really known me, my commitment or my calling.[79]

The King who disobeys the law in the name of Black emancipation can only operate on an authority that is higher than Black emancipation, legitimate and pressing as that cause may be. Vietnam might serve Black interests in America, but the interests of Black Americans, no matter how impatiently awaited, no matter how urgently needed after 340 years of waiting for "constitutional and God-given rights," are not the issue. The issue is justice, abstractly conceived: That's the only authority that stood above the Supreme Court in Birmingham, and it cannot be advanced by turning a blind eye on the destruction of another people "the world over" to promote the interests of Black Americans.

Fellow civil rights leaders felt betrayed. Whitney Young, of the National Urban League, complained, "Johnson needs a consensus. If we are not with him on Vietnam, then he is not going to be with us on civil rights."[80] *The New York Times* agreed, condescendingly writing that King was making "too facile a connection" between civil rights and war politics, and so did *The Washington Post*, arguing that King "diminished his usefulness to his cause, his country and his people."[81] No doubt, most of these critics attacked King because they wanted to further civil rights in America, not just the war. Their mistake, however, Black or white, was the same as that of "white moderates." They could not fathom King's "calling" because unlike King they had forgotten the meaning of the Declaration of Independence. King's duty was to the idea that all men are created equal, not "his country" or "his people"—regardless of whether the people were

"Americans" or "Blacks." He was seeking justice, not the insertion of African Americans into the American "union." A hundred years earlier, Thoreau and Emerson would have understood King's "calling"—his "appointment," or "genius." Kant, too, would have understood why he had to jeopardize the African American rights and interests for which he fought and died. Not just liberty can assassinate. Emancipation can assassinate, too. If universalism would be betrayed in its name, the authority of justice would be even more badly deformed, and the mark of Cain would remain an open wound.

Truth, Enemy of the People

We hold these truths to be self-evident, that all men are created equal.

—THE DECLARATION OF INDEPENDENCE

Truth about an independent metaphysical and moral order cannot [. . . provide a] basis for a political conception of justice in a democratic society.

—JOHN RAWLS

1.

IMMEDIATELY AFTER DONALD TRUMP took the president's office for the first time in 2017, the hostilities between his administration and the media evolved into a conflict about facts, or truth. Tensions ran high well before Inauguration Day, for the incoming president had campaigned with what many interpreted as a discourse of bullshit, in the strict philosophical sense of the term—that is showing no interest in truth *or* falsity.[1] But at some point, it became increasingly clear that Trump was moving from bullshit to a system of organized lying. Kellyanne Conway's claim that the White House would provide "alternative facts" is now remembered as a symbolic moment; the term she coined perseveres as Trumpism outlasts Trump's presidency. Her later justification of the Muslim ban by invoking a nonexistent "Bowling Green Massacre" signaled that the situation was escalating, as did Steve Bannon's denunciation of the media as the "opposition party" to what Trump called "the movement."[2] Soon thereafter, the president himself tweeted that the media, insisting as it did on truth, was not *his* enemy but the "enemy of the American people."[3]

Mainstream media retaliated swiftly with aggressive moves of their own. Newspapers started bringing their fact-checking procedures, which previously remained behind the scenes, ostentatiously to the fore. By now, it is common practice for news outlets to print such titles as "Fact Check: President Trump's First Week" or "Fact Check: President Biden's Address to Congress."[4] As if to threaten with strategic weapons, *The New York Times* announced in 2017 that it had reconsidered its unwritten "L-word" policy.[5] Previously, editors at the *Times* maintained that lying depended on an internal state of mind—an intention to deceive—that could not be verified. Accordingly, they preferred terms such as "falsehoods," "untruths," or "errors" instead of "lies." Ever since

Trump was elected, however, the verb "to lie" has been printed. The *Times* also ran for long months this advertising slogan: "Truth. It's vital to democracy. No alternatives, just facts. Get up to 40% off the *Times* subscription of your choice." In a similar vein, after the January 6th storming of the Capitol, social media platforms such as Twitter and Facebook, which were scolded for spreading misinformation, suspended and even permanently banned activists' accounts—including that of the outgoing president.

This crusade in the name of facts says it all. It shows not just how fragile truth is in liberal democracy but what truth's limits are: As facts are fervently defended, the idea of justice is depleted of authority. To be sure, the media's campaign in defense of facts certainly is vital to democracy. But we should notice how keen news outlets have been to declare a holy epistemological war. Arguably, the sanctification of facts serves to conceal deeper questions about truth and its relation to politics, to subdue the suspicion that truth in a more meaningful sense of the term has been suppressed. When Trump labeled the liberal media as the "enemy of the people," many were outraged. But the relation between truth and politics is more complex than his liberal opponents would like to concede. Not just populist nationalist politicians are attacking truth with weaponized "fake facts"; not just postmodern leftists, equipped with the latest theory of postcolonialism or critical race. When politics is not about facts but about justice—when moral truth contradicts comfortable consensus—modern liberals treat truth as just that: the enemy of the people.

"Take care of freedom, and truth will take care of itself." Richard Rorty liked repeating this slogan to capture the essence of modern liberalism. The idea is to radicalize religious toleration by an overriding principle of state neutrality.[6] Thomas Jefferson once said of religion, "it does me no injury for my neighbor to say that there are twenty Gods or no God."[7] For the author of the Declaration of Independence, it was necessary to privatize faith to preserve the authority of truth: All men are equal, regardless of religion. Modern liberalism might seem at first to extend Jefferson's principle by privatizing not just faith but truth itself. In the same way that the state ought not impose a religion on its citizens, it has no right to promote a concept of justice. Just as politics was freed from the authority of God, it was also "liberated" from the authority of truth: not merely factual truth but truth understood as an independent principle of justice that stands above the will of the people. On a second look, this isn't a radicalization of Jefferson's principle but goes directly against it. While religion was privatized to affirm the authority of truth, the privatization of truth undermines its very authority. Liberalism thus consists, to use another apt slogan by Rorty, in the "priority of democracy to philosophy."[8]

Another way to understand this transition is to notice that while Jeffersonian toleration sacrificed the Mosaic distinction (the claim that there is no God but God) in the name of the Abrahamic distinction (the claim that there is only the authority of justice), modern liberalism sacrificed both. Whereas the Declaration of Independence averred an absolute principle of a justice that is not man-made and politics must follow, modern liberalism celebrates a "new conception of what it is to be human" and has "no room for obedience to a nonhuman authority."[9] In other words, the only absolute principle is human will.

The most effective way to undermine the impact of truth on politics is not to attack facts but to fetishize them. Wittgenstein famously claimed that "the world is the totality of facts," and deduced from this claim that, in the world, "everything is as it is, and everything happens as it does happen: *in* it no value exists."[10] In a world exhausted by facts, "it is impossible for there to be propositions of ethics": All meaningful statements are of "equal value," so ethics "cannot be put into words."[11] The point is not so much that propositions such as "all men are created equal" aren't confirmed by facts; it is that they can be neither confirmed nor falsified by them. Once facts are elevated as the model of meaningful assertions, therefore, ethical propositions are degraded to, at best, myths, ideologies, or subjective opinions. Strictly speaking, they are deemed nonsensical. Liberalism as we have come to know it is so comfortable with this fact fetish for the same reason that it goes against Kant's idea of humanity and returns to the positivist Enlightenment that preceded him—it lives only where duty to moral truth has been replaced by consensus, interest, and opinion.

To appreciate the predicament that is caused by this replacement, it is worth considering the relation between truth and politics more generally. While politics is the realm in which powers and wills are negotiated, truth is indifferent to the influence of both: Not even the most powerful of tyrants nor the most legitimate of democracies could decide that two plus two equals five. If truth ever does influence politics, therefore, it can only be imposed on the political realm from without. In political terms, the question is whether human powers, wills, and authorities should be guarded not just by constitutions, checks and balances, and international treaties—they all belong to the political realm and bend to its principles—but also determined by truth's external authority. Tyrants' obsessive aspiration to undermine truth is due to their inability to accept any such external imposition on their wills. But before we get too comfortable with the familiar comparisons—from Hitler to Stalin, from Trump to Putin, from Fascism to Nazism—it's worth noticing that modern liberalism relates to truth much like tyrants do: by rejecting its authority over the sovereign's will—in this case, the people's. A "new concept of man" that rejects "all obedience to nonhuman authority" may sound like an emancipatory progress of secular Enlightenment modernity, but it leaves one wondering on what authority disobedience to human authority can ever be pursued. Hans Frank, Bavaria's minister of justice and *Reichsminister* under Hitler, once formulated the totalitarian relation to truth thus: "as the pursuit of knowledge is the service of truth, it must necessarily be service to National-Socialism."[12] To oppose this totalitarian formula, the authority of truth must remain independent. It is hardly a good idea to accept Frank's logic and only replace "National-Socialism" with "democracy." This is exactly what the celebrated "priority of democracy to philosophy" and the "new concept of man" has to offer.

2.

Paradoxically, the historical watershed that undermined truth as a political power was the American Civil War. It was fought in the name of an absolute truth, and, in the name of such truth, slavery was abolished. A legal text like the US Constitution was revised because a metaphysical concept of justice was enforced by violence. For a brief moment, abolitionism prevailed in American politics—but only for a moment. In the immediate aftermath of the war and in response to its horrors, truth was discarded, abolitionism was abolished, and unionist thinking became the driving force of liberal politics. Democracy is still hostage of this unionist triumph.

It is common nowadays, in some circles, to deny the war's abolitionist moral motivation and dismiss the North's cause as mere economic interest, coupled with the refusal to accept the South's secession.[13] By the same token, it is emphasized that the Emancipation Proclamation of January 1, 1863, pronouncing "free" all persons "held as slaves," only liberated those held captive in the rebellious states and only as a war necessity: It was meant to undercut the South's economy, which relied on slave labor as white Confederacy citizens were fighting.

Of course, it is useless to deny that such motives existed and were weighty. But whatever truth there is in this description of the war, it disregards what the soldiers who fought the war—who killed and died—thought that they were fighting for. W. E. B. Du Bois, who did more than any other author to expose the North's ulterior economic motives, also goes out of his way to emphasize that the idea that "the whole North during and after the war was chiefly interested in making money, is only half true."[14] To "ignore abolition is unhistorical. In growing ascendancy for a calculable time was a great moral movement which turned the North from its economic defense of slavery and led it to Emancipation. Abolitionists attacked slavery because it was wrong and their moral battle cannot be truthfully minimized or forgotten."[15] This tradition had to be appreciated in order to uphold what Du Bois, receiving the Lenin Peace Prize at the Russian embassy in Washington, identified as the "dream of America," an "abolition democracy" that respects those very principles that made it obligatory for the Union to go to war.

True, the North's battle cry was *Union!* not *Abolition!* This can be misleading: The North was fighting under the banner of union because the South had seceded, and the South seceded because the country had elected for president a man like Abraham Lincoln. He was no abolitionist in spirit, but still a proponent of the idea that the Declaration of Independence must be placed above the Constitution; that self-evident truth must prevail over the will of the people or what was called back then "federal consensus." The growing abolitionist sentiments in the North are best testified by the fact that the same soldiers who were shouting "Union!" on the battlefield were also singing "John Brown's Body" as their marching hymn:

John Brown's body lies a-mouldering in the grave,
John Brown's body lies a-mouldering in the grave,
John Brown's body lies a-mouldering in the grave,
His soul is marching on.

[...]
Now, three rousing cheers for the Union,
Now, three rousing cheers for the Union,
Now, three rousing cheers for the Union,
As we are marching on![16]

Only a few years earlier, Brown was denounced by unionists and abolitionists alike as insane. The memory of the abolitionist who took the law into his own hands to uphold the Declaration of Independence and was the first US citizen to be executed for treason—with Lincoln's public approval—was marching on as the Union's spirit.

No less expressive of that spirit was Lincoln's Gettysburg Address in 1863. To our ears, it may sound like a laconic affirmation of democracy as the "government of the people, by the people, for the people." Taken out of context, the slogan may sound as uncontroversial as Martin Luther King Jr.'s claim that an unjust law is no law at all. To Lincoln's audience, the position he articulated in two hundred and fifty words as the war was still raging was more meaningful.

The ceremony was conceived from the start as a performative act, a dedication of the war's bloodiest battlefield to the memory of the Americans who fell on its ground. In his speech, Lincoln took up that theme, *dedication*, but after rolling multiple variations of it on his tongue concluded that the site cannot be dedicated at all. Rather, the nation must dedicate itself anew to the same truth to which it was pledged at its founding. "Four score and seven years ago our fathers brought forth, upon this continent, a new nation, conceived in liberty, and dedicated to the proposition that 'all men are created equal....' Now we are engaged in a great civil war, testing whether that nation, or any nation so conceived, and so dedicated, can long endure."[17] To a crowd of Northerners, caught throughout the antebellum years in the heated debate between abolitionism and unionism, the message was clear. At Gettysburg Lincoln did not avow democracy in some general sense of that term; he dedicated the nation to a particular understanding of it. The speech is not just a repudiation of the South's alleged right to own slaves, it is a rejection of unionism as the answer to the South's claim. The country is to be given "a new birth of freedom" by reenacting its commitment to the Declaration of Independence. To the priority of truth over consensus, of metaphysics over the constitution.

This was clear enough from Lincoln's words, but it was made clearer by the setting. The speech dates November 19, more than four months after the battle that had raged in Gettysburg in early July. Approximately 7,000 Americans were killed on that ground in less than three days of fighting—some 3,100 Union Northerners and 3,900 Confederacy soldiers. They were all buried together in a rush at the battlefield, for the quick decomposition of bodies posed an immediate threat to public health. Once fall came, and it was decided to undertake a second burial and a presidential "hallowing" of the ground, the bodies were excavated and separated: The remains of Confederate soldiers were to be sent to their home states rather than dignified at the new national memorial. A meticulous process of identification and separation of bodies started in October and would not end before the spring of the following year. And so, as Jonathan Lear writes, it is not too much of an exaggeration to say that when Lincoln arrived at the site, he had to "watch his step."[18] As the American president avowed democracy and gave the nation a "new birth in freedom," thousands of American bodies were lying bare—Confederate bodies excluded from dignified burial. And Lincoln, the history reader, orator, and indeed performer, was certainly aware of them.

Insofar as the Union fought the war for unity, this gruesome spectacle makes no sense at all. Why not bury fallen Confederacy soldiers side by side with fellow Northern soldiers, let alone allow the humiliating presentation of their bodies at the primordial moment of America's unified second founding? "The unburied dead were fighting to withdraw from common citizenship with those who killed them," Lear writes.[19] "The Union soldiers who killed them did so in the name of insisting that they, the Confederates, as well as their loved ones and descendants, must remain fellow citizens," he argues, lamenting the failure to bury fellow Americans as Lincoln's "Antigone moment."[20] The ghosts of Gettysburg allegedly still haunt the American union today.

However, since Lincoln's act at Gettysburg was his way to performatively determine the war's cause, Lear's account is begging the question. Contrary to his assumption, the war was not fought primarily to include Confederacy soldiers as fellow citizens. Arguably, that was just the point that Lincoln was making in his anti-unionist words *and* deeds. Union soldiers were fighting to emancipate Blacks and include all men in "the people," not to keep Southern citizens as members of the union. The country that gave itself a "new birth in freedom" at Gettysburg by dedicating itself to truth cannot dedicate Gettysburg to soldiers who fought to deny it—the truth that all humans must belong to the people is upheld by the Confederate soldiers' exclusion. The mark of Cain is healed by a duty to humanity, not by pretending that all Americans are brothers.

Gettysburg's spirit did, for a moment, prevail. On January 31, 1765, the Thirteenth Amendment passed: What the Emancipation Proclamation had announced in a limited way and as a matter of war necessity was now asserted as a matter of principle. In April of the same year the war ended, and an era of Reconstruction started, with the politics of radical or congressional Reconstruction, continuing the abolitionists' war goals by other means. Political battles were raging, making progress in achieving what was anything but consensual or commonsensical: For one thing, that freed Black slaves would be indeed incorporated as citizens. For another, that Black citizens would be able to vote. But this spirit was quickly overturned. The war that abolished the institution of slavery also swiped away the intellectual atmosphere that made abolitionism possible. In the war's immediate aftermath, as a direct reaction to the traumas of its horrifying cost, unionist principles returned with a vengeance. Liberal democracy as it emerged from the war asserts the "priority of democracy to philosophy" and the wish to "take care of freedom and let truth take care of itself," that is, the exact opposite of the principle that Lincoln attempted to reenact at Gettysburg. He asked to give the nation a "new birth in freedom" by dedicating it to truth, and thought that this priority must be upheld if a government "of the people, by the people, for the people, shall not perish from the earth."[21]

3.

The revolution of the mind (more accurately: counterrevolution) is clearest in the thinking of Oliver Wendell Holmes Jr. The legendary Supreme Court justice and founding father of American pragmatism started the war as an abolitionist. He fought bravely and was seriously wounded three times, only to return again and again to combat. His father, Holmes Sr., was a close associate of Ralph Waldo Emerson, who was the author of "Self-Reliance" and Holmes Jr.'s godfather and mentor. In one nonconformist essay of his student years, Holmes Jr. drew the ire of his Harvard professors by writing that "duty" would not have been "less binding had the Bible never been written, or if we were to perish utterly tomorrow."[22] In other words, it is a necessary truth that transcends both revealed religion and the world's physical existence. "Do men own other men by God's law?" Holmes Jr. asks in another Harvard paper; "when we, almost the first of young men who have been brought up in an atmosphere of investigation ... when we begin to enter the fight, can we help feeling it is a tragedy? *Can we help going to our rooms and crying that we might not think?*"[23] This isn't merely abolitionist language; it is the type of abolitionism that Emerson propagated along with Thoreau, identifying the toleration of slavery with unionists' conformist mentality or a childish failure to think for oneself. In 1860, soon after Lincoln's election to the presidency, Holmes Jr. took on a job as bodyguard to Wendell Phillips, a prominent abolitionist orator from Boston who became an outspoken supporter of John Brown and scarcely escaped a kidnap attempt by proslavery activists as he was on the way back from his funeral. One evening in

Boston, Holmes Jr. was busy guarding Phillips at a rally as his own godfather, Emerson, set the crowd afire arguing from stage: "The monstrous concession made at the formation of the Constitution ... has blocked the civilization and humanity of the times up to this day."[24]

Holmes returned from the war convinced of exactly the opposite. The transformation of his thinking turned on the idea of truth and the authority of universalism. He did not stop believing the idea that all men are equal, but he came to despise the thought that any idea bears authority, or entails a duty, let alone an absolute one. He came to believe that certitude in normative truth promotes barbarism rather than civilization. A self-evident concept of justice was no different from that other metaphysical certitude, faith, that had led to the Thirty Years' War and only ended by the tolerant privatization of religion.

Holmes's extension of toleration from faith to justice was corroborated by Darwinism, which had begun gaining prominence in the years of the war. His Darwinian idea was that thinking is nothing but a tool, an experiment put forward to test our environment. In a perfect match of content and form, this included the idea of humanity itself: Humans are created by blind evolution, so their thinking can posit no higher thought. They themselves are not worthy of some absolute dignity. "I detest a man who knows that he knows," Holmes wrote in a letter to his friend Harold Laski. It is always the idea of truth through which one group compels another to conform to its own idea of justice: "Some kind of despotism is at the bottom of seeking for change . . . I don't care to boss my neighbors and to require them to want something different from what they do—even when, as frequently, I think their wishes more or less suicidal."[25] From an Emersonian abolitionist Holmes became a unionist constitution-alist, and started elaborating the philosophy that sustains this ideology, namely pragmatism. "You respect the rights of man," he writes in another letter to Laski, "I don't, except those things a given crowd will fight for—which vary from religion to the price of a glass of beer. I also would fight for some things—but instead of saying that they ought to be I merely say they are part of the kind of world that I like."[26]

> Your remark about the "oughts" and system of values in political science leaves me rather cold. If, as I think, the values are simply generalizations emotionally expressed, the generalizations are matters for the same science as other observations of fact. If, as I sometimes suspect, you believe in some transcendental sanc-tion, I don't. Of course, different people, and especially different races, differ in their values—but those differences are matters of fact. . . . I have very little respect for the conventions in them-

selves, but respect and generally try to observe those of my own environment.[27]

The man who once claimed duty was binding even if the Bible had never been written and the world ceased to exist now translates all norms as statements of fact, reducing expressions of first-personal duty to descriptions of interests and conventions. His godfather once wrote that believing "what is true for you in your private heart is true for all men" is "genius," and associated that with Brown.[28] Holmes now detests the person who "knows that he knows" and must be thinking of the same person.

Or, in fact, not just of Brown, nor even just of the abolitionist movement, but of the spirit that for a moment marched through the Union.

In an early decision that would become his trademark as a judge, Holmes replaced that spirit with the naturalist belief that "a man rightly prefers his own interest to that of his neighbors."[29] This principle became the staple of his defining work, *The Common Law.* "The *ultima ratio*, not only *regum*, but of private persons, is force, and that at the bottom of all private relations ... is a justifiable self-preference"; the law thus "pretty nearly corresponds ... with what is then understood to be convenient."[30] It is not surprising that a book of this sort would be written in 1881, just a few years after Reconstruction was ended by the Compromise of 1877, which followed the same logic: privilege the interests of liberal white voters in the North over the basic rights of emancipated slaves. It marked the country's fall from Reconstruction, with its lasting abolitionist undercurrents, into almost a century of Jim Crow legislation that would not end until the 1960s with Martin Luther King Jr. In 1896, the US Supreme Court upheld racial segregation, or what came to be known as the doctrine of "separate but equal," as constitutional. Holmes was not yet sitting on that court's bench, but his *Common Law*, anchoring the idea that law can only be based on "the prevalent moral and political theories, intuitions . . . even the prejudices which judges share with their fellow-men" is representative of that zeitgeist.[31] More accurately, a zeitgeist that dismisses the application of principles that stand above the zeitgeist: "Men to a great extent believe what they want to," Holmes writes. "*I see in that no basis for a philosophy that tells us what we should want to want.*"[32] The Nietzschean-Spinozist idea that we don't "desire anything because we judge it to be good" but judge it to be good "because we desire it" could not have been endorsed more clearly.[33] Judge Richard Posner once summarized Holmes's position, pointing out, approvingly, that he turned law "into dominant public opinion in much the same way that Nietzsche turned morality into public opinion."[34] Opening his 1918 Harvard lecture "Natural Law," Holmes indeed repudiated the idea that man, that "little creature on this little earth," can claim for any norm the status of a "cosmic truth."[35] The similarity to Nietzsche's mockery of values in our "remote corner of the universe" is almost certainly not coincidental.[36] Morality, Holmes goes on to argue, is nothing but the expression of the perspective of the world's victors: "Certainly we may expect that the received opinion about the present war will depend a good deal upon which side wins."[37] In 1918, this is conveniently interpreted as a comment on the First World War. But as some Harvard students in the audience must have realized, the meaning of this general principle, especially coming out of Holmes's mouth, must be tested as a comment on the Civil War. With a lot of goodwill, this reduction of justice to the victor's morality can be interpreted as embracing unionism. A more accurate interpretation would be the claim that, had the Confederacy won, our views on Black slavery would have looked more like John Calhoun's and less like Abraham Lincoln's.

Holmes's most significant student was John Dewey, and it is not much of an exaggeration to say that, through Dewey, liberal thinking inherited Holmes's Nietzschean unionism rather than the legacy of Lincoln's Gettysburg. In Dewey's terms, the project was to create a "philosophy of liberalism" that would take over once the "inheritance of absolutism" has been "eliminated."[38] By "absolutism," he means the idea that a self-evident truth should determine politics. Holmes's *The Common Law* opened with a well-known paragraph claiming that the "life of law," or its authority, depends on contingent cultural convention rather than truth. He terms these conventions "experience":

> The life of the law has not been logic: it has been experience. The felt necessities of the time, the prevalent moral and political theories, intuitions of public policy, avowed or unconscious, even the prejudices which judges share with their fellow-men, have had a good deal more to do than the syllogism in determining the rules by which men should be governed.... [The law] cannot be dealt with as if it contained only the axioms and corollaries of a book of mathematics.... The substance of the law at any given time pretty nearly corresponds, so far as it goes, with what is then understood to be convenient.[39]

Dewey's lifelong project can be interpreted as a footnote to this paragraph. He espouses its replacement of truth by cultural convention, or "experience," and extends that notion from the realm of law to a comprehensive theory of liberal democracy. *Experience and Nature*, Dewey's major opus, ends with expansive borrowing from Holmes's aforementioned lecture "Natural Law" and Holmes, reading it in old age, complained that the work was too inelegantly written but added: "So methought God would have spoken had He been inarticulate but keenly desirous to tell you how it was."[40] In *German Philosophy and Politics*, written in 1915 as a commentary on the First World War, Dewey had already argued against all transcendent values, writing that "philosophical absolutism" may be "as dangerous as . . . political absolutism" and went out of his way to ascribe the origins of German nationalism to Kant.[41] The key to understanding "the mind of Germany," he writes, is the distinction Kant draws between "nature" and "freedom" in order to defend a transcendent metaphysics that asserts a categorical duty as a "supreme law of action."[42] It is remarkable that the dignity of humanity as a categorical truth, labeled here as "absolutist" and despised by the father of modern American liberalism as characterizing the "German mind" from Kant to Bismarck (presumably all the way down to Hitler), is actually an American tradition stretching from the Declaration of Independence via abolitionism to Lincoln.

In the same essay, Dewey construes Nietzsche as the democratic alternative to Kant's "absolutism" and, as such, as the democratic antidote to the nationalist tradition that goes back to his thinking. If Nietzsche's allegedly democratic rejection of all absolute values—including the dignity of humans—as slave morality has its own nationalist undertones, Dewey was careful to exonerate him. And if these nationalist undertones themselves went hand in hand with anti-Semitism, then apparently the type has valid philosophical reasons—Jews were the ones who introduced monotheism, the ground of "absolutism," into the world. As Rorty would later put it, "Dewey might well have agreed with Nietzsche that 'Monotheism...the faith in one normal god beside whom there are only pseudo-gods—was perhaps the greatest danger that has yet confronted humanity.'"[43]

The rejection of absolute universal values has everything to do with Dewey's relation to the Civil War. Publicly, he said little, if anything. Sidney Hook, Dewey's longtime student and associate, commented on his private position:

> There is one theme related to violence that Dewey never wrote about at length, so far as I know, but that nonetheless lay close to his heart.... This was the American Civil War, in whose shadow or aftermath he came to critical self-consciousness.... Dewey believed there was no historic necessity for the Civil War, although he recognized that after John Brown's raid at Harpers Ferry, it was too late for Lincoln's solution, which was to liberate the slaves by purchase. Dewey was no admirer of John Brown, and he felt that Emerson, whom he greatly admired...was acting out of character in his extravagant defense of Brown. Dewey felt that Lincoln's solution would have cost less even in money than the actual cost of the Civil War [...], not to speak of the hundreds of thousands of lives lost and the immeasurable human suffering, the bitter legacy of Reconstruc-

tion, and of the exacerbated situation since.[44]

Behind this position is Dewey's principle of the "identity of ends and their means." Democratic goals, he argues, can only arise from democratic procedures: compromise, negotiation, deliberation, persuasion—not disruption, revolution, or war. This principle provides in turn the underpinnings of Dewey's "reformative" as opposed to "revolutionary" left. Democrats, he thought, must pursue amelioration through social organization, judicial battles, and legislation rather than conflict. However, while there is no doubt that social organization is immensely significant—Dewey is rightly remembered as a cofounder of institutions like the NAACP and ACLU—his reformative politics properly understood was not the alternative to "revolutionary" politics but to the abolitionist tradition. The idea that slaves should have been emancipated by negotiation and *purchase*, liberating them in a long process of compensation to slave owners, tax reductions to Southern states that diminish slavery, and so forth—reinforces the assumption that four million humans were in the first place owned by right. Apparently, democracy can grow for Dewey from the nonviolent idea that humans can own humans, not from the violent means by which this assumption was abolished.

If Reconstruction failed to achieve equality in the aftermath of the Civil War, it wasn't because democratic ends cannot be achieved by the radical universalism of the abolitionists. It is because unionism much like Dewey's triumphed immediately after, and equality cannot find a footing where one human may own another by right. Those who think democracy can tolerate that notion would also negotiate and compromise the rights of freed men. King wrote in Birmingham that the one thing worse than using "immoral means to attain moral ends" is using "moral means to preserve immoral ends."[45] He certainly was not thinking consciously of Dewey. But when King denounces "white moderates" for posing a greater obstacle to emancipation than white supremacists by preferring "order" over justice, he is arguing from the absolutist position that Dewey's "new concept of man" attempted to eradicate. The principle in whose name eight white clergymen denounced King in an open letter as an "outside agitator" is just that: a plea not to disturb "common sense" or Deweyan "experience" by King's "eternal law."

Whereas King's metaphysical position proceeds from the Declaration of Independence and is continuous with Du Bois's abolition democracy, Dewey gave us unionist democracy. For Du Bois, abolition democracy denotes the ambition to construct a democratic tradition that continues the same moral commitment that led to the war. For Dewey, the idea was to eliminate the metaphysical idea of man that called for the war and replace it with the common sense, or experience, that would have prevented it in the first place. Speaking of the tendency among intellectuals of his age to denounce Reconstruction as the failure of radical Black politics, Du Bois commented: "One fact and one alone explains the attitude of most recent writers toward Reconstruction; they cannot conceive Negroes as men."[46] Indeed they couldn't, not because of some theory of race that emerged from bad science and not from Enlightenment universalism coupled with Kant's ugly comments in his side lectures on anthropology, but because of a philosophy that was backed by Darwinian science and undermined humanity in the first place. Once liberalism discarded the Kantian idea of men as absolutist and metaphysical, humans no longer commanded the categorical dignity that the idea entails. For the comfortable majority this may be fine, for their humanity is most of the time taken for granted. Minorities are thereby stripped of the "abstraction" that commands higher authority than the majority's common sense, shared experience, interests, or consensus-based legitimate laws. And the irony, or tragedy, is that mistaking unionist democracy for Kantian universalism, progressives dispose of the idea of humanity instead of reclaiming it.

4.

The debates about "identity politics" may seem a recent phenomenon, but they go back to the 1990s, and Dewey's unionist reformism has informed the attack on identity all along. Identity liberals, the argument goes, have given up on the locution "we Americans" or "we the people" as the anchor of politics. As a result, instead of promoting pragmatic agendas that could unify the country around the urgent needs of its middle class, the identarian left resorts to moral hysteria, interpreting structural injustices as personal moralistic imperatives. The result is pseudo-politics: a retreat from genuine public engagement to secluded philosophy departments in which society is dissected into a celebration of difference and victimized identity groups. In *Achieving Our Country*, a celebrated liberal manifesto that asked to revive "leftist thought in twentieth-century America," Rorty urged progressives to ditch French postmodernism, which gained prominence during the "culture wars," and replace it with Dewey's reformist pragmatism. Only such reformism, exemplified in programs like Roosevelt's New Deal, could ensure unity rather than difference and guard American "national pride." If pride and unity were lost, Rorty warned, "something will crack"; Americans would "start looking around for a strongman to vote for—someone willing to assure them that, once he is elected, the smug bureaucrats, tricky lawyers, overpaid bond salesmen, and postmodernist professors will no longer be calling the shots."[47] When twenty years after *Achieving Our Country* was published, Trump got elected wearing a red Make America Great Again hat—and American progressives were caught up in endless battles over the latest theory of intersectionality, postcolonialism, gender studies, and critical race—many returned to Rorty as a rediscovered oracle.

Mark Lilla's familiar attack on identity in *The Once and Future Liberal*, based on his widely read *New York Times* op-ed "The End of Identity Liberalism," set the tone of this return to Rorty.[48] Lilla never mentioned Rorty by name, and he wouldn't qualify his thinking as a "leftist" vision for the twenty-first century. But, for better or worse, this was the most elaborate attempt to counter identity by reviving Rorty's Deweyan ideal of patriotic reformism. According to Lilla, American political history in the last century can be told as the rise and fall of two political "dispensations," each providing its own "catechism" and inspiring a different vision of "America's destiny."[49] First, a Rooseveltian era, stretching from the New Deal of the 1930s to the late 1960s, which promoted a political agenda based on "citizenship." Second, a Reaganite era, consisting not in liberal but in libertarian politics. Undoing everything that Roosevelt had been about, it stressed individualism over "solidarity" and entrepreneurship over citizenship or "collective action." It is only appropriate that this libertarian era culminated with the figure of Trump, an "opportunistic, unprincipled populist."[50]

Progressives, the argument goes, did not spend the last forty years developing an alternative vision for America's "shared destiny."[51] Instead, they joined the decomposition of politics into anti-political "elementary particles," turning liberal politics itself into a stage for pseudo-political drama where action had been replaced by personal "self-expression."[52] This "narcissistic," "reactive," "resentful," "disuniting" approach could not but alienate the majority of American citizens.[53]

Lilla has been denounced by at least one author as a "white supremacist," but this only supports his claim that current proponents of identity prefer the "purity" of propositions over their "truth." Anyone who is familiar with the atmosphere on American campuses and in other intellectual circles would have to lend his argument an ear. In the years following the heated debates over Lilla's intervention, as Trumpism became mainstream, identity lingo became more aggressive, polarizing, and extreme.

One early example of the current identity complex was the dispute that erupted in 2017 over *Open Casket*, a painting by the artist Dana Schutz. Depicting the mutilated body of Emmett Till, a Black child, it was presented at the Whitney Biennial at the Whitney Museum of American Art and sparked outrage—a white artist allowed herself to work on Black suffering.[54]

The background story requires comment. In August 1955, Till, who grew up in Chicago, visited his great-uncle in Money, Mississippi, for a summer vacation. Early on August 28, he was abducted, tortured, and eventually executed by white men who had accused him of having spoken disrespectfully to a white woman. The open-casket funeral, held in Chicago by Till's mother, Mamie Till-Mobley, saw tens of thousands of mourners in attendance. *The Chicago Defender* printed an image of Till's casket, forcing the American and international public to witness in his body the barbaric face of the America that had failed Reconstruction and preserved Jim Crow laws. There was also an international dimension: As American liberalism was in the thick of its Cold War competition with Soviet Russia over the paradigm of equality and justice, the image of Till's deformed body gave liberal democracy a bad face. In one 1963 sermon dedicated to Mother's Day, Martin Luther King Jr. spoke of the "crying voice of a little Emmett C. Till, screaming from the rushing waters in Mississippi."[55] King's "I Have a Dream" was delivered at the feet of Lincoln's massive statue at the Lincoln Memorial, facing hundreds of thousands who had joined the March on Washington for Jobs and Freedom on August 28, 1963—eight years to the day after Till's death.

Schutz's *Open Casket* is a large painting of the original image in *The Chicago Defender*. Its aesthetic effect is created by the painful blending of matter and form: The distinction is blurry between the shattered perspective—Schutz often paints parts of her subjects from different angles—and Till's broken body. The work's naïve colors—also characteristic of Schutz—give the impression of a desperate attempt to bestow childlike happiness on the fourteen-year-old boy from the black-and-white photograph. The work's aesthetic success is a matter of controversy, but this is beside the point. The point is that Schutz is white, and a manifesto drafted by the Black artist Hannah Black called upon the Whitney's curators to remove the painting. Signed as a petition and circulated broadly, the letter contained an "urgent recommendation that the painting be destroyed" for exploiting "Black pain" for art as "raw material":

> That even the disfigured corpse of a child was not sufficient to move the white gaze from its habitual cold calculation is evident daily and in a myriad of ways, not least the fact that this painting exists at all. In brief: the painting should not be acceptable to anyone who cares or pretends to care about Black people because it is not acceptable for a white person to transmute Black suffering into profit and fun. . . . Although Schutz's intention may be to present white shame, this shame is not correctly represented as a painting of a dead Black boy by a white artist— those non-Black artists who sincerely wish to highlight the shameful nature of white violence should first of all stop treating

Black pain as raw material. The subject matter is not Schutz's; white free speech and white creative freedom have been founded on the constraint of others, and are not natural rights. The painting must go.[56]

The term was not yet in use, but the manifesto gave the cue for subsequent "cancel culture" controversies. And indeed, if *Open Casket* must go, one can compose a long catalog of forbidden artworks that should stand in line for removal, not to say destruction—arguably with Gerhard Richter's Birkenau cycle high on the agenda. By the standards of the manifesto, this set of paintings, a German "appropriation" of a Jewish perspective from within Auschwitz's gas chamber—in fact, a German "gaze" painting over it, erasing it—can easily be portrayed as a use of Jewish suffering as "raw material."[57] For the time being, the work is presented in the foyer of the Reichstag.

Schutz's *Open Casket* remained in the Whitney Biennial, accompanied by a written explanation. She cannot "know" what it is like to be "black in America," Schutz expounded, but she does "know what it is like to be a mother," and "Emmett was Mamie Till's only son."[58] In other words, Schutz fully endorsed the principles of her critics but invoked her own identity as a woman and a mother to legitimize her art. It is not much of an exaggeration to say that, in this sense, she could have added her name to the petition that called for her work's destruction. She accepted the premise that if she hadn't had some allegedly adequate identity, the painting might have "had to go."

The only way to salvage Schutz's work from this logic is to remind both the artist and her critics that neither Black nor female nor Jewish experience can be owned. Those in the habit of complaining about "appropriation" only reveal their assumption that human suffering can be used by its rightful owners as "raw material." The problem with this logic is that whatever can be owned by someone can be owned by anyone, the main question is the price. Only a compromised understanding of human pain can create the instrumental assumption that because I'm Jewish, I can have a right to know Jewish suffering, and own—not to say use it.[59] To be sure, the fact that no human pain can be owned does not imply that it cannot be the subject of art. To the contrary, it must be handled through artistic creation, the one medium of human activity that has a chance to transcend the prevalent reduction of thinking to instrumental use. In the embarrassingly honest wording of the manifesto against *Open Casket*, transcending such instrumental logic is not something that art can accomplish—it is but a tool for "profit and fun."

In other words, both Schutz and her critics have to be reminded that the author, like God, is dead. If there is such a thing as art, then it is possible only because artists are not authorities over the meaning of their creation. In the era of identity, however, the author is anything but dead. Everything is about the author; the meaning of her work is thoroughly determined by the horizon of her concrete biological, conventional, and historical perspective. Once, the author's deconstruction was perceived as an emancipatory move that had the power to liberate texts and thereby whole cultures from hegemonic authorities that determined their meaning. For a Michel Foucault or a Roland Barthes, the question "who speaks" seemed obscene; we have come full circle to a culture that fetishizes that query—this is the prime interest of art and everything around it. Who speaks, and by what right.

Could Schutz answer her critics that she painted Emmett Till as a human being? Could she say that as a white person she doesn't know what it's like to be Black in America, and that she cannot know what it was like to see and show your child's dead broken body—not even as a mother (and how presumptuous of any artist to think they might just by being Black)—but that she asks to reach to an experience that isn't hers in order to create an art that, like humans, cannot be reduced to knowing and using as "raw material"? The relation between art and human freedom was once just that: an attempt to overcome a factual conception of truth, to transcend the unsatisfactory alternative between facts and fake facts that dominates our instrumental relation to the world, to seek an experience that is not bound to one's private identity, experience, interest, perspective. And yet here is the point: The impossibility of such prior human perspective is the underlying assumption that is shared by both identity progressives and their liberal critics.

To understand this continuity, it is worth taking a look at Barthes's "The Death of the Author."[60] At first, the French postmodern title may seem to put forward an anti-universalist, anti-Enlightenment thesis, and this may well be what Barthes himself thought he was doing. The essay, however, goes not against the Enlightenment but against a particular strand of the movement—the positivist strand that undermined universalism. Barthes is right to point out that whereas pre-Enlightenment societies did not attach significance to authors as authorities, Enlightenment "positivists" discovered their prestige. For earlier societies, authors were shamans or prophets—at most, their "performance" was admired, while they themselves were only mediators, assigned by a higher calling that was not *theirs*. Enlightenment naturalism canceled the possibility of such higher assignment, reducing art back to the individual: It was "only logical" that this trend, "the epitome and culmination of capitalist ideology," came to place the "greatest importance to the 'person' of the author."[61]

However, by reducing meaning to the person of the author, Enlightenment positivism culminates as a relativist ideology.

Meaning is never universal; it is forever attached to the author's identity. What Barthes does not realize is that Kant, like Barthes, was a critic of the Enlightenment's delegation of final authority of the text to the author. Theodor Adorno captures this point in his lectures on Kant's *Critique of Pure Reason* by saying that enlightenment depends on rejecting "that disastrous word 'as,'" the clause you meet "when people say in the course of a discussion '*As a German*, I cannot accept that . . .' or '*As a Christian*, I must react in such-and-such a way in this matter.'"[62] When Barthes claims that writing is "the negative where all identity is lost,"[63] he formulates a condition of universalism against Enlightenment positivism. The destruction in writing "of all points of origin"— of the author's identity, which Kant would have called his *private* perspective—is a condition of public thinking, that is as universal as thinking for oneself. That's the perspective that the identarian left *and* the Deweyan liberals deny. All thinking is, in that view, private; the idea of moving beyond the horizon of one's contingent historical conventions, intuitions, histories, prejudices, desires, or language that Dewey calls "experience" is rejected by both sides as an "abstract" and "metaphysical" fiction.[64]

5.

And so, especially if we take seriously the threat posed to thinking by its reduction to identity, we must also question the allegedly universalist alternative that the liberal critics of identity claim to offer. In Rorty, we fall back on a replacement of abstract humanism by something "local and ethnocentric," the body of shared conventions, depending on "national pride," that determine the sense of the word "we."[65] In Jill Lepore, liberalism is similarly salvaged by making "The Case for the Nation," and, in Lilla, there's "no liberal politics without a sense of *we.*"[66] The only answer to populist demagogy on the one side and postmodern identity on the other is recourse to "something that as Americans we all share but which has nothing to do with our identities."[67] Undermining the "universal democratic *we* on which solidarity can be built," Lilla complains, progressives have been "unmaking rather than making citizens."[68] "*We* is where everything begins."[69]

This is the core of liberals' alternative to identity, but it is also their greatest liability. After the truth that unified humanity was discarded, the difference between we-liberalism and identity politics is no longer sharp. Kant would have agreed with the critics of liberalism that once the abstract concept of humanity is rejected, a post-metaphysical reincarnation of unionist politics is itself but a form of identity politics: not of Black people, LGBTQ+ people, feminists, or members of other minorities, but of all those who are comfortable enough to open a political debate by the locution "we Americans," "we Germans," "we Israelis."

For true universalists, "we" ought never be where politics *begins*; it can only be its open-ended result. For politics when it matters the most is the debate over—and, sometimes, a war on—who gets to be included in this "we," or "the people," with the American Civil War being only the most obvious example. Universalist politics must consist in changing who "we" are, how "we" will come to understand our values, not in relation to our past identities, values, and histories but in relation to a duty to truth that transcends our interests, intuitions, and convenience—and will determine who we will be in the future. That was the meaning of Lincoln's gesture at Gettysburg, as he gave the nation a "new birth" by changing its identity according to truth. And that is just the move that is rejected by the identarian left and the liberal center as metaphysical.[70]

Lilla seems at least half conscious of this problem, for he repeatedly modifies the words "we" and "citizen" by the adjective "universal." And, in brief, irritated footnotes, he tries to dismiss the question of who counts as a citizen as a "sign of how polluted our political discourse has become."[71] Polluted or not, that's the question that reveals his "universalist" critique of identity as itself identarian. The word "we" is never universal; patriotic politics is not cosmopolitan politics. By the same token, "universal citizenship" is a contradiction in terms. In short, liberalism is not humanism: Those who now speak of a universal "we" are those who are privileged enough—that seems to be the right term—to forget that their stress on "we" was in the first place devised to eliminate the duty to humanity.

The same betrayal of universalism entraps John Rawls's liberalism. It boasts an idea of justice that is "political, not metaphysical," and therefore furnishes a framework for unionist democracy that begins with a "we" and is relevant to "us."[72] "Philosophy as the search for truth about an independent metaphysical and moral order," Rawls writes, cannot "provide a workable and shared basis for a political conception of justice in a democratic society."[73] A metaphysical "moral order" is then replaced by consensus. "Since justice as fairness is intended as a political [that is, not metaphysical] conception of justice for a democratic society," he writes,

it tries to draw solely *upon basic intuitive ideas* that are embedded in the political institutions of constitutional democratic regime and the public traditions of their interpretation. Justice as fairness is a political conception in part because it starts from within a certain political tradition. We hope that this political conception of justice may at least be supported by what we may call "overlapping consensus," that is, by a consensus that includes all the opposing philosophical and religious doctrines likely to persist and to gain adherents in a more or less just constitutional democratic society.[74]

If Rawls is perceived these days by both enemies and friends as a Kantian universalist, that's because we have drifted far away from a genuine meaning of the concept. His substitute of truth by consensus, achieved by mediating the "intuitions" of those who speak "from within a certain tradition" is the most muscular replacement of Kant's abstract duty to humanity by Dewey's naturalized shared experience. Our intuitions are nothing but *facts* about us, incapable of determining duties that are not grounded in our "tradition"—that is, our identity. Rawls's idea of overlapping consensus is nothing but the most prevalent way in which democracy becomes prior to philosophy, and "local and ethnocentric," convictions that determine the sense of the word "we," become prior to a universal idea of justice. His "political, not metaphysical" slogan is probably the greatest expression of unionism's triumph over abolitionism, and over Gettysburg and the Declaration of Independence.

In the antebellum years, Emerson and Thoreau claimed that such unionism goes hand in hand with conformism of the sort that Alexis de Tocqueville had warned about in *Democracy in America*. According to Tocqueville, a tyranny of the masses threatens to ensue once the "theory of equality" is "applied to minds."[75] Where all thoughts are of the same value, false ones are as good as true. But since an independent standard of truth contradicts this equality, it is eliminated, replaced by what everyone can agree on—in other words, consensus. The result is the conviction that there is "more enlightenment" in a "group of men" who agree among themselves than in the thinking of one, or the few, who might follow truth and contradict common opinion—these are dismissed by this reasoning as fanatic.[76]

The danger of such conformism, Tocqueville points out, is that it allows the majority's wishes to be enforced not just by physical threats or state power—as old-fashioned tyrants went about imposition—but as legitimate authority. Once the higher metaphysical authority of truth is denied, the only standard that *can* bestow legitimacy is what everybody can agree on—at least, all those who are included. Such internalized moral authority can determine not just what people say, or do, but what they think and will—a level of controlling the multitudes that old tyrants could not have dreamed of achieving. In a passage that Adorno and Horkheimer would pick up as a pillar of their *Dialectic of Enlightenment*, Tocqueville comments,

> Formerly tyranny employed chains and executioners as its crude weapons; but nowadays civilization has civilized despotism

itself. . . . Princes had, so to speak, turned violence into a physical thing but our democratic republics have made it into something as intellectual as the human will it intends to restrict. Under the absolute government of one man, despotism, in order to attack the spirit, crudely struck the body. . . . But in democratic republics, tyranny does not behave in that manner; it leaves the body alone and goes straight to the spirit.[77]

Emerson and Thoreau knew well that as these lines were written, bodies in America were anything but "left alone." Millions of slaves were held not just by the power of the whip but by norms, and a rule of law, that drew legitimacy from conformism.

But in current political, philosophical, sociological reality? How does the doctrine of the "equality of minds" gain prominence if not through the privatization of truth? What is the tyranny of the masses if not the idea that justice is replaced by "overlapping consensus" while excluding independent justice as "metaphysical" and hence unsuitable for "modern democratic societies"? After decades of unionist dominance over liberal thinking, Tocqueville's description of the sociological powers that would lead the American mind to the tyranny of the masses is infused into philosophy by Rawls's very method.

In "Who Are We?," a short essay from 1996, Rorty spells out the consequences of such "we-liberalism" particularly honestly.[78]

Once we overcome Kant's abstract concept of humanity, he argues, the question of our identity becomes the fundamental question of philosophy. It is the one question that "has always already been answered when we answer other questions."[79] Instead of justifying our politics against absolute oughts, we turn to justify ourselves in relation to the "body of our shared belief" that Rawls called "intuitions" and Dewey "experience."[80] What we will and will not do to achieve equality or justice, whom we will include or exclude in our conversation about this, is itself determined by justifying ourselves to those who "always already" share it with us. Quoting from Posner, Rorty explains,

> Judge Posner wrote that "The very high crime rate of young black [American] males is an aspect of the pathological situation of the black underclass, but there do not appear to be any remedies for this situation that are at once politically feasible and likely to work. In the context in which Posner writes, "politically feasible" means "compatible with the fact that the American middle class will not let itself be taxed to save the children of the underclass." This unwillingness creates a situation in which those children cannot hope for a decent chance in life. To predict that unwillingness will persist is to say that there will, in the future, no longer be any "we" which unites the political class of the US and those underclass children in a moral community.

Those black children are no longer, if Posner's judgment of political feasibility is right, among "we, the people of the United States," any more than their slave ancestors were when the US Constitution was written.[81]

With this statement, unionist democracy from Holmes to Rawls comes into its own. Just as unionists would not have sacrificed life, money, and the wealth of the American market to emancipate Blacks that in their common sense and intuition were in any case inferior, we-liberals cannot think of a duty to change their lives to "save children of the underclass." If truth once stood above consensus to obligate the American middle class, that's the absolutist assumption that liberalism has eliminated. Rorty goes on to extend this vision globally:

> Suppose that there is no imaginable way to make decent life-chances available to the poorer five billion citizens of the member states of the United Nations while still keeping intact the democratic socio-political institutions cherished by the richer one billion.... Then they will begin to treat the poor and unlucky five billion as surplus to their moral requirements, unable to play a part in their moral life. The rich and lucky people will quickly become unable to think of the poor and unlucky ones as their fellow humans, as part of the same "we."

Those who make the decision about feasibility are answering the question "Who are we?" by excluding certain human beings from membership in "We, the ones who can hope to survive." When we realize that it is unfeasible to rescue a person or a group, it is as if they had already gone before us into death. Such people are, as we say, "dead to us." Life, we say, is for the living.[82]

The measure of feasibility is our own identity, embodied in our way of life. And it is to us that we answer the question of what living standards we might jeopardize, and for whom; whether we will keep Black children as part of the American people (or not); and who will count globally as a fellow human. The mark of Cain was never borne more comfortably. Life, we say, is for the living: *Am I my brother's keeper?*

The Abraham Distinction, or What Enlightenment Is

It really is the complete opposite, so to speak, of obedience! Each person is a lawgiver. In Kant, nobody has the right to obey.

—HANNAH ARENDT

1.

IMMANUEL KANT'S ANSWER TO the question "What is Enlightenment" is well known. "Enlightenment," he writes, is "man's emergence from his self-imposed immaturity"; immaturity, he adds, is "the inability to use one's own understanding without the guidance of another."[1] This definition has become so prevalent that it is now difficult to doubt or question it, difficult to feel a need to scrutinize its meaning. But since the freedom to think for oneself provides in Kant the ground of humanity's absolute worth—his definition of humanity in moral rather than biological terms—it is perplexing that the question isn't raised more often, if at all: What counts as using one's own understanding? What counts as thinking for oneself?

The straightforward answer Kant provides in the text—thinking for oneself is refusing another's authority over our thinking—is plausible but, providing a merely negative criterion, hardly sufficient. It only tells us what thinking for oneself is not. Perplexity is increased by two exclamation marks that Kant builds into the text, emphasizing that the negative definition he provides contains no description but a command. "*Sapere aude!* Have courage to use your *own* understanding!"[2] Anyone who is not a child of the Enlightenment, in the worst sense of the term, must wonder: Does following *this* command count as thinking for oneself?

To start appreciating the significance of Kant's claim that Enlightenment is using one's own understanding "without the guidance of another," it is important to notice its continuity with Spinoza's definition and rejection of prophecy in the *Theological-Political Treatise*. Prophecy, Spinoza writes, is "certain knowledge about something revealed to men by God." A prophet is "someone who interprets things revealed by God *to those who cannot themselves achieve certain knowledge of them*."[3] Spinoza begins the *Theological-Political Treatise*—the opening shot of what some call the radical Enlightenment—by addressing prophecy and repudiating it because he, too, defines Enlightenment as rejecting the authority of others over our thinking. On a first look, then, Spinoza and Kant define Enlightenment in the same way: It is refusing to orient our thinking by the authority of another—another who is then, by Spinoza's definition, a prophet.

A careful look at Kant's concept of Enlightenment reveals that this continuity is misleading. It is often remembered that immaturity, for Kant, is the tendency to comfortably forfeit thought by outsourcing it to others: "If I have a book that has understanding for me," he writes, "a pastor who has a conscience for me, a doctor who judges my diet for me, I have no need to think, if only I can pay; others will take over the tedious business for me."[4] However, it is often overlooked that Kant warns in the essay of another kind of immaturity, one that's deeper and more pernicious to Enlightenment. Strictly speaking, this type of immaturity is not a form of nonthinking or of outsourcing of thought; it is rather *a way* of thinking—a way of using our reason in a dead or mechanical way. It is the use of "rules and formulas," Kant writes, "these mechanical instruments of a rational use (or rather misuse) of [man's] natural gifts, [that] are the fetters of an everlasting immaturity."[5] The danger that we would make it our habit, exactly when we do think, to fall back on pre-given, mechanical algorithms, is more dangerous to independent thinking than simply outsourcing thinking to others.

"Mechanical instruments of a rational use"—arguably the best way to understand the "everlasting fetters" Kant has in mind is by reference to what Alexis de Tocqueville analyzed as the tyranny of the masses. The tendency to conform—falling back on others' pre-given standards of thought—replaces the ability to think freely by a mechanical application of these standards. Once the true and the good are determined by what many consent to, internalized as the way to determine legitimacy, external authority is imposed from within and *Selbstdenken* becomes virtually impossible. Kant has such internalized imposition in mind when he sees the danger of "mechanical" thinking becoming a habit, or quasi second nature. If that's our condition, immaturity is in some sense not even self-imposed—"for the present" one is "really incapable of using his reason." The greatest threat to Enlightenment then is not some violent external imposition but this unique "achievement" of the masses' tyranny, rendering thinking people into "domestic cattle."

It is in view of this threat that Kant, immediately after issuing his command to think for oneself, argues that most people cannot achieve this on their own. He claims that Enlightenment must first be achieved by "only a few" who succeed, "through the exercise of their own minds," to rid themselves of the "yoke of immaturity."[6] If and *only if* these unique few then "disseminate among the herd the spirit [*Geist*]" of appreciating both "individual worth and the vocation of each man to think for himself" can Enlightenment be achieved by the public.[7] It turns out that for most people, using their own understanding without the guidance of others depends on following the example of others—Enlightenment, faced by the threat of the tyranny of the masses, depends on some form of prophecy after all. In 1859, Henry David Thoreau could still complain that journal editors prove their conformism by dismissing John Brown as insane for claiming he had been "appointed."[8] Ralph Waldo Emerson's idea of genius was a reference to the same untimely notion, namely following genius, or the capacity to follow "your own thought," as "true for all men." And if we tolerate Martin Luther King Jr.'s speaking of his "calling," it is because we domesticate him by assuming he isn't quite serious about that "calling" himself. But it's worth noticing that Brown and King are quite like the "unique few" Kant is talking about when he says individuals would have to "throw the yoke" of conformism on their own and spread the "spirit" of human worth and thinking for oneself. Enlightenment thus depends in some sense not on a rejection of prophecy but on a translation of that notion. Kant's modernization of the idea of prophecy provides his most mature account of what Enlightenment is. But then, what is prophecy?

2.

Providing a philosophical answer to that question may seem obsolete now, but it once stood at the heart of philosophical speculation for the simple reason that prophecy was taken to convey truth. Moses Maimonides, the greatest rationalist Jewish authority of all time, provided a definition of prophecy in *The Guide for the Perplexed*. "Prophecy," he writes, is "an overflow overflowing from God ... through the intermediation of the Active Intellect, toward the rational faculty in the first place and thereafter toward the imaginative faculty. This is the highest degree of man and the ultimate term of perfection that can exist for his species."[9] It is the gift of the imagination rather than the intellect that is the fundamental condition of prophecy, and not everyone can have it:

> This is something that cannot by any means exist in every man. And it is not something that may be attained solely through perfection in the speculative sciences and through improvement of moral habits, even if all of them have become as fine and good as can be. There still is needed in addition the highest possible degree of perfection of the imaginative faculty in respect of its original natural disposition.[10]

The key role of the imagination in prophetic "assignment" is not arbitrary. Whereas scientific knowledge of facts is determined by objects that are given to the senses, cognition through the intellect (that is, conceptual cognition) is determined by rules of thought. The imagination is thus the only faculty whose operation is not determined by given objects or prescribed norms. This freedom may cause error and illusion—it often does—but it also renders it a source of experiencing what lies beyond mere truths of fact. As Leo Strauss once commented, "since imagination can function independently...there exists the possibility that the [deity] may force imagination into its service for perceiving the super-sensory: hence the possibility of prophecy."[11]

As the main prophetic faculty, the imagination is for Maimonides also "the political faculty par excellence."[12] It enables the prophet not just to be appointed by higher calling but to communicate that calling successfully to the masses. The question is how one understands this communication. And, on a common view, which is often ascribed to Maimonides, prophecy is nothing but giving God's law to the people. Maimonides, it is generally thought, considered Moses, who initiated monotheism by delivering the Decalogue to the Hebrews down from Mount Sinai, as the supreme prophet. This identification in turn determines the nature not only of prophecy but of monotheism, the origin of universalism—which was announced by that prophecy. The Decalogue is a set of written commandments that opens with a series of monotheistic decrees ("You shall have no other Gods before me") and was imposed on freed slaves, demanding obedience. This logic goes hand in hand with the so-called Mosaic distinction or the "price of monotheism," namely the idea that faith in this exclusive deity gives rise to an intolerant absolute authority that taints monotheism as the dangerous imposition of absolute law that Nietzsche dismisses as slave morality.[13]

However, this long-standing tradition of interpretation is off the mark. Moses is not Maimonides's or the Bible's supreme monotheist prophet. Biblical monotheism is not just the discovery of a uniquely true deity and imposing that deity's law is not what prophecy is.

The first cause for doubt that the giver of the Decalogue is Maimonides's prime prophet comes from the biblical text. Maimonides's "official" position is that Moses, unlike the other prophets, prophesized without requiring the mediation of the imagination—he saw God directly. This claim, however, is awkward. The evidence in the biblical text does not just fail to bear it out but refutes it, describing Moses's prophecy in the very same figurative, imaginative language that is typical of all prophets.[14] Moreover, it is plainly stated in the Bible that no mortal can see God and survive. Maimonides could not have failed to remember—and could not expect his sophisticated readers to forget—that this ban was dictated to none other than Moses himself, who asked to see the deity directly and was rebuffed: "You cannot see my face, for no one may see my face and live."[15]

This discrepancy between *The Guide for the Perplexed* and the biblical text is significant. Maimonides opens the book with a warning to the reader that the book's true doctrine, like the Bible's, is concealed.[16] The overt ("exoteric") position he spells out directly is only intended for the masses; the truth doctrine has to be uncovered by those capable of tracing the contradictions and hints in his argumentations, using them to deduce his true position by comparing different chapters and reconstructing the book's hidden ("esoteric") truth. His relation to Mosaic monotheism, then, seems to be a case in point.

This suspicion grows once we consider Maimonides's classification of the degrees of prophecy.[17] The eleventh and highest prophetic degree he names is one in which "a prophet sees an angel speaking" in a prophetic vision.[18] Maimonides then asks— without mentioning Moses—whether there is another, higher degree of prophecy; whether "it is possible that a prophet would also see *in a vision of prophecy* that God, as it were, addressed him."[19] And he rules this out: "This, in my opinion, is improbable, for the power of the act of the imagination does not reach this point. And we have not found this state in any of the prophets."[20]

It is remarkable that this statement contradicts again Maimonides's overt position about Moses, who allegedly did see God directly. At the same time, *this* statement is actually in perfect harmony with the biblical text, where the impossibility of seeing the deity directly was explained to Moses himself. Maimonides's classification of prophetic degree implies that Moses's prophetic category, which would have been the twelfth and highest, does not in fact exist—he seems to belong to a lesser prophetic category, of those who see God but in a mere dream rather than a vision. Which, in turn, deconstructs Moses's role as the supreme monotheist prophet and the common understanding of what monotheism may seem to be about.

This conclusion is strengthened by the fact that Maimonides also positively tells us, in the same chapter of *The Guide for the Perplexed*, what the Bible's supreme example of prophecy is. Immediately after defining the highest prophetic state as that in which the prophet sees "an *angel* who addresses him *in a vision*," Maimonides adds: "as *Abraham at the time of the binding* [of Isaac]. In my opinion this is the highest of the degrees of the prophets whose states are attested by the prophetic books."[21] If not Mosaic but Abrahamic, what is prophecy?

Assuming the common reading of the Binding of Isaac, the answer may seem obvious and disturbing. Abraham, the story goes, provides a model of unquestioning faith. The idea would seem to be that from the monotheistic notion of a uniquely true deity follows the commitment to absolute obedience. The deity's command introduces a suspension of the ethical.[22] Nothing, however, could be further from Maimonides's position. To see this, it is necessary to return to his interpretation of the Binding of Isaac.

Recall, Maimonides wrote that seeing an angel in a vision is the highest prophetic degree, to which Genesis 22 testifies: "the prophet [sees] an *angel* who addresses him *in a vision*, as *Abraham at the time of the binding*." The biblical narrative begins when God (Elohim, אלוהים) addresses Abraham in speech, commanding him to sacrifice Isaac: "and God tested Abraham, and said to him 'Abraham' and he said 'Here I am'; then He said 'Take your son, your only son Isaac, whom you love, and go the land of Moriah and offer him there for a burnt offering upon one of the mountains which I will show you."[23] We know that hearing this command from God doesn't stand for the highest manifestation of prophecy. Hearing God is on the *Guide*'s taxonomy an inferior prophetic degree, and in any case it isn't what Maimonides had in mind when evoking the Binding of Isaac to exemplify the "highest of the degrees of the prophets," which consists in an appearance of an angel. Indeed, later in the narrative an angel directly addresses Abraham. Remarkably, it is not the angel of God (Elohim) but of Yahweh (יהוה)—the angel who commands him at the last moment before slaying his son to stop the sacrifice. One must ask here, as the rabbis repeatedly have, by what authority Abraham decides to follow the angel's command rather than God's. The question is especially appropriate because this angel is the angel of Yahweh, while it was God (Elohim) who had given the initial decree. And one must in any case wonder why, according to Maimonides, it is in virtue of doing just that, following the angel of Yahweh rather than hearing God (Elohim), Abraham presents the supreme prophetic degree.

The answer to this question is found in Maimonides's theory of divine names. It is well known that the biblical stories use different words to signify the deity. Maimonides holds that Yahweh (יהוה) denotes the deity's proper name, while the word "God" (Elohim) is a merely equivocal term. Originally signifying rulers and judges of states, it came only derivatively to signify deities.[24] More specifically, since deities sometimes serve as judges, they are referred to as Elohim. The essential signification of "God," then, is nothing but the attribute of juridical authority: the law of the state, the common norm of the land, determined by contingent conventions.

The implications of this view become clearer in light of Maimonides's interpretation of the story of the Fall.[25] The serpent in the story claims that by eating from the forbidden fruit, Adam and Eve would become "like God [Elohim], knowing good and evil,"[26] and it is tempting to read this as: They'll become divine-like by gaining ethical knowledge. But Maimonides interprets the story exactly the other way around. He claims that gaining God-like knowledge of good and evil represents the *punishment* imposed on Adam and Eve. Coming to know like God (Elohim) is losing the higher knowledge of truth possessed in the Garden of Eden—coming to think and judge through contingent, conventional norms and rules, depending on a mere man-made socio-historical context:

> When man was in his most perfect and excellent state, in accordance with his inborn disposition and possessed of his intellectual cognitions . . . he had no faculty that was engaged in any way in the consideration of generally accepted things. . . . [However], he was punished by being deprived of that intellectual apprehension . . . becoming endowed with the faculty of apprehending generally accepted things, he became absorbed in judging things to be bad or fine. . . . Hence it is said: *And ye shall be like Elohim knowing good and evil;* and not: *knowing the false and the true,* or *apprehending the false and the true.*[27]

Apply this to Maimonides's account of the Binding of Isaac and, thereby, of prophecy. God (Elohim) commands Abraham to sacrifice his son. This signifies obedience to conventional man-made authority, falling prey to the all-too-human tendency to conform to what society accepts as if a just decree. Indeed, and this is the point, sacrificing one's firstborn to God *was* following the ethical and the legal norm in Abraham's pagan Near East. Blatantly immoral commands can be, and often are, taken for the right thing to do, legitimized by consensus and constitutions. Abraham exemplifies the greatest degree of prophecy by obeying not God—that is, conventional norms—but the ethical authority standing above them. Abraham's supreme prophecy consists in managing the truth rather than consensus—defy God and sacrifice the ram instead of the son.

Moreover, by going against the common norm Abraham does not merely disobey. He sets a model of disobedience that can be followed by his sons. Maimonides explains this point with a powerful interpretation of the meaning of the Binding of Isaac as a test or a trial. He goes to great pains to argue that the word "test" (*nisayon*, ניסיון) in the verse "after these things, and God tested [נסה] Abraham" does not stand for God attempting to *examine* Abraham (obviously, God knows what Abraham will or will not do).[28] Rather, Abraham is tested in order to be presented as an example, a standard to be disseminated by his followers. The notion of trial consists not in "the accomplishment of a particular act" commanded by God but rather in a story becoming "*a model to be imitated and followed.*"[29] The Hebrew root of "test" (*nisayon*) can be both n-s-y (נ.ס.י), standing for "examined," or n-s-s (נ.ס.ס), standing for "presented as an emblem or a model." (When a flag or a symbol is exhibited, in Hebrew it *mitnoses*.) In this light, Genesis 22:1 can also be translated as: after these things, God exhibited Abraham as an example. Abraham's supreme prophecy can be seen as the primordial example of enlightenment: of those who throw off the "yoke of immaturity" and "disseminate among the herd the *Geist*" of appreciating both "individual worth and the vocation of each man to think for himself."

3.

If we now return to the text of the Binding of Isaac, we can see that the idea that Abraham turns against God rather than obeys him is no Maimonidean invention. The insistence that justice transcends any authority is Abraham's original innovation. Biblical monotheism does not consist in the claim that there is one, uniquely true deity—an idea that with Sigmund Freud or Jan Assmann can be interpreted as an Egyptian achievement that Moses imported to freed Hebrew slaves.[30] It consists rather in subjecting even that uniquely true deity to moral law, an intellectual innovation of a different order than the faith in one deity that's announced in the Decalogue—and one that is completely

137

foreign to Moses. Once we understand the original story of the Binding of Isaac, we can appreciate biblical ethical monotheism and the universal idea of man as a being that's open to absolute law, by the Abrahamic distinction.

The outline of the Binding of Isaac is well known. God commands Abraham, "take your son, your only son, Isaac, whom you love, and go to the land of Moriah and offer him as a burnt offering."[31] Abraham wakes up early the following morning and starts the journey. After three days, he "lifts up his eyes" and sees "the place which God had shown to him from afar."[32] Abraham continues to walk with Isaac and his servants until they reach the mountain pointed out by God. Abraham commands his servants to wait there: "Stay here with the donkey; the boy and I will go to the mountain to worship, and then we'll return to you."[33] Abraham gives the wood for the altar's fire to Isaac and together they begin to climb as Isaac says, "Father," and Abraham answers, "here I am, my son."[34] "Here is the fire and the wood" for the altar, "but where is the Lamb for the burnt offering?"[35] Abraham's answer is: "*Elohim Yir'e lo ha'se le'ola, bni*" (השה לעולה, בני אלוהים יראה לו).[36] Translation can hardly do justice to this answer: "God will provide to himself," "see for himself," "show himself," or "find out for himself the Lamb for the burnt offering"—all are possible translations of the Hebrew. Eventually, father and son reach the place that God had shown Abraham. This is where the crucial scene begins—the moment that was visualized for generations by Rembrandt, Caravaggio, and Chagall:

[9] Then they came to the place of which God had told him, and Abraham built an altar there, and placed the wood in order and he bound Isaac his son and laid him on the altar upon the wood; [10] And Abraham stretched out his hand and took the knife to slay his son; [11] But an angel of the Lord called to him from heaven and said "Abraham, Abraham" so he said "Here I am" and he said "Do not lay your hand on the lad or do any harm to him; [12] for now I know that you fear God, since you have not withheld your son, your only son, from me"; [13] And Abraham lifted up his eyes and looked and behold behind him was a ram caught in a thicket by its horns; and Abraham went, and took the ram, and offered it up for a burnt offering instead of his son; [14] And Abraham called the name of the place God-will-see, as it is said to this day in the mountain of the Lord it shall be seen [15] Then the angel of the Lord called to Abraham a second time from heaven; [16] And he said "By myself I have sworn, says the Lord, because you have done this thing and have not withheld your son, your only son [17] blessing I will bless you and multiplying I will multiply your descendants as the stars of the heaven and as the sand which is on the seashore; and your descendants shall possess the gate of their

enemies; [18] in your seed all the nations of the earth shall be blessed because you have obeyed my voice; [19] and Abraham returned to his young men and they rose and went together to Beersheba; and Abraham dwelt in Beersheba.[37]

Interpreters traditionally ascribe the story to the biblical author E (standing for the Elohist). This is due to the fact that the story uses almost exclusively Elohim (אלוהים), God, for the deity, and because it has obvious parallels to other characteristic E stories. On that reading, the second angelic speech made to Abraham in verses 15 through 18, occurring after the trial had ended and Abraham sacrificed the ram "instead of his son," is a later interpolation into the text. Those verses use Yahweh (יהוה), the Lord, for the deity, not God (Elohim), and their style and composition is poetic and repetitive—in sharp contrast to the rest of the narrative, which is noted for its harshly economic use of language. Moreover, if one simply skips those textually anomalous verses, the sentences continue to flow coherently, and the grammar and narrative remain undamaged. This is telling, especially considering that this text is probably the most concisely formulated narrative in the Hebrew Bible. One important biblical interpreter referred to this second angelic speech as nothing but a "clumsy addition" to what is otherwise a "beautifully written story."[38]

More recently, however, biblical scholars observed that this explanation cannot be quite accurate. They point out that Abraham's obedience necessitates some kind of blessing or reward, some response from God, which Abraham only receives in the second angelic intervention. It is unconvincing, therefore, that the angel's speech was simply inserted at a later point into the narrative. What happens in those verses—textually irregular though they may be—is in fact indispensable for the *meaning* of the narrative, namely Abraham's obedience.

We face, then, a contradiction between two well-founded observations. On literary and philological grounds, it seems that the second angelic speech simply doesn't fit. At the same time, this speech is necessitated by the content of the story—Abraham must be rewarded for his obedience. For some, this suggested that accounting for the original text is impossible. As one prominent scholar wrote, there may have been "a simpler, shorter account of the sacrifice of Isaac, but to identify the original account with verses 1–14 is too simple, for the author responsible for verses 15–18 also left his mark on verses 1–14, so that identifying the limits and content of earlier versions of the story is elusive."[39]

In fact, such identification is possible, and the confusion about it in the literature provides the main cue. We need to notice that verses 11 and 12—where the angel makes his first appearance, stopping Abraham at what seems to be the very last moment before he kills his son—exhibit the same textual anomalies as the second, "interpolated" angelic speech. Verses 11 and 12 use "Lord" (Yahweh, יהוה) rather than "God" (Elohim, אלוהים) for the deity; their style is repetitive and poetic in contrast to the rest of the text, which is economical; and if we simply skip those verses, which come at what presents itself as the very climax of the narrative, we find that its logic and the style flows undamaged. (In fact, as we shall see, they improve.) But the narrative that emerges on this reading turns out to be very different from the one we have taken for granted:

[9] Then they came to the place of which God had told him, and Abraham built an altar there, and placed the wood in order and he bound Isaac his son and laid him on the altar upon the wood; [10] And Abraham stretched out his hand and took the knife to slay his son; [13] And Abraham lifted up his eyes and looked and behold behind him was a ram caught in a thicket by its horns; and Abraham went, and took the ram, and offered it up for a burnt offering instead of his son.

[9] וַיָּבֹאוּ אֶל הַמָּקוֹם אֲשֶׁר אָמַר לוֹ הָאֱלֹהִים, וַיִּבֶן שָׁם אַבְרָהָם אֶת הַמִּזְבֵּחַ, וַיַּעֲרֹךְ אֶת הָעֵצִים; וַיַּעֲקֹד אֶת יִצְחָק בְּנוֹ, וַיָּשֶׂם אֹתוֹ עַל הַמִּזְבֵּחַ מִמַּעַל לָעֵצִים [10] וַיִּשְׁלַח אַבְרָהָם אֶת יָדוֹ, וַיִּקַּח אֶת הַמַּאֲכֶלֶת לִשְׁחֹט

אֶת בְּנוֹ [13] וַיִּשָּׂא אַבְרָהָם אֶת עֵינָיו, וַיַּרְא וְהִנֵּה אַיִל אַחַר נֶאֱחַז
בַּסְּבַךְ בְּקַרְנָיו; וַיֵּלֶךְ אַבְרָהָם וַיִּקַּח אֶת הָאַיִל, וַיַּעֲלֵהוּ לְעֹלָה תַּחַת בְּנוֹ.

In the original narrative, Abraham ultimately disobeys God's command, sacrificing the ram "instead of his son" by his own decision. The interpolated figure of an angel takes out of Abraham's hand not just the knife but the responsibility for stopping the trial: It takes a story that culminates in Abraham's ethical disobedience as the symbol of faith and makes it into one that celebrates obedience. In a classic interpretation of this story's style, Erich Auerbach argued that this narrative characteristically avoids any "externalization" of internal states of mind. It demands interpretation from readers, he noted, by providing only action, no explanation—allowing the "externalization of only so much of the phenomena as is necessary for the purpose of the narrative, all else left in obscurity."[40] This is true, but not of the figure of the angel: As it alleges to stop Abraham at the very last moment, it spares no effort to explain in dramatic terms that Abraham agreed to kill his son: "Do not lay your hand on the lad or do any harm to him, for now I know that you fear God, since you have not withheld your son, your only son, from me."

We can, it seems, not just resolve the contradiction in the scholarly literature but understand its source. The second angelic intervention indeed is a later interpolation, just as much as it is necessitated by Abraham's obedience: the obedience that was in the first place manufactured by the interpolation of the angel's figure. As Maimonides, too, seems to have realized, the angel of Yahweh marks the difference between two levels of meaning in the text. An external one and an original one. The former, familiar to us, conveys the idea of absolute obedience to God. The latter, forgotten, asserts the idea that Abraham's ethical disobedience is the true meaning of his faith.

Two more observations are in order. The first still concerns the text itself. The Binding of Isaac is famously formulated along a fast and laconic stream of verbs, connected to each other by *vav-ha'hibur*, standing in biblical Hebrew for either "and" or "but." The author uses this sequence of verbs to create the tension of the story, as was again stressed by Auerbach: "And they *came*, and Abraham *built*, and he *placed* the wood, and *bound* Isaac, and Abraham *stretched forth* his hand."[41] At this point, the angel interrupts the laconic sequence, using long sentences and poetic language to celebrate Abraham's alleged intention to kill his son: "But an angel of the Lord called to him from heaven and said 'Abraham, Abraham' so he said 'Here I am' and he said 'Do not lay your hand on the lad or do any harm to him; for now I know that you fear God, since you have not withheld your son, your only son, from me." On a first read, this seems reasonable. If this is the climax of the story, then it is only natural that the angel interrupts the accelerating stream of verbs. The tension of the narrative must be resolved rather than continue to rise—and indeed, the angel resolves the tension dramatically, by saving Isaac.

But note how the narrative continues once the angelic figure has finished its intervention. The stream of verbs accelerates, and with it the tension: "And Abraham *lifted up* his eyes, and *looked* and *behold*, and Abraham *went*, and *took*, and *sacrificed*." There are five more action verbs here, which is relatively more than in the stream of verbs preceding the angelic intervention. We find here a clause with the verb *va'isa et eynav* (וישא את עיניו), "and he lifted up his eyes," which in biblical narrative often describes a protagonist experiencing the story's turning point. We also encounter the word *ve'hine* (והנה)—literally "and here" or "and now," signifying much abruptness (it could be translated as "suddenly"). This is awkward. Was not the tension of the narrative already resolved by the intervention of the angel? If at that point Isaac has already been saved, why does the tension not only fail to wane in what follows but so obviously increases?

The answer is that in the original narrative the tension had not yet been broken; the verbs continue to accelerate up to verse 10: "and they came to the place which God had told him, and Abraham built an altar there, and placed the wood in order, and he bound Isaac his son and laid him on the altar upon the wood."

This tension continues to build into verse 13, the story's original turning point: "but Abraham lifted up his eyes, and looked, and behold behind him was a ram." Only then does the tension break, collapsing with no explanation, just action, by Abraham saving his son: "and Abraham went, and took the ram and offered it up for a burnt offering instead of his son."

The second observation is rather a question; namely is it reasonable to assume that Abraham would disobey a direct divine command? Asked differently, is it reasonable to assume that biblical monotheism as it was understood two thousand years ago would present a concept of faith that seems so modern about man's relation to God? It is only with Kant, one might think, that modernity learned to question authority based on the principle that authority depends on ethics.

But we already know the answer to that question, because it leads us back to Genesis 18 and the story of Sodom. There, Abraham speaks as a prophet who is at once more radical but more modern than any other—contesting not a king but God—in the name of justice. Immediately after he learns of God's plan to destroy the city, Abraham "steps forward" (the Hebrew word is *va'igash* (ויגש), which implies to approach aggressively, almost with a threat) and says: "Will you also destroy the righteous with the wicked? ... Far be it from you to do such a thing as this, to slay the righteous with the wicked, so that the righteous should be as wicked; far be it from you. Shall not the judge of all the earth do what is just? . . . Now that I have taken it upon myself to speak to the Lord, though I am nothing but dust and ashes . . . Will you destroy the whole city?"

Asking whether biblical monotheism can be so "progressive" as to express ethical disobedience is asking the wrong question. More adequate is to ask whether the same Abraham who carries out this speech in Sodom can silently bind his son on the altar. The idea of duty to speak up to the highest authority in the name of justice is intertwined with Abraham's humanity: He "took it upon himself" to speak to the lord as a mere human ("I am but dust and ashes"). His humanity derives from consciousness of absolute law: not a law of God but the same law to which he subjects God, too. Kant would articulate the same point in his analysis of the Sublime, in the *Critique of Judgment*, writing that "to fear God and to be afraid of him are not the same thing. We are afraid of God when we transgress and feel guilty; we fear God when we so dispose ourselves that we are ready to stand before him."[42] Kant applies that idea of the fear of God, turned into the sublime, when commenting on the Binding of Isaac:

We can use, as an example, the myth of the sacrifice that Abraham was going to make by butchering and burning his only son at God's command (the poor child, without knowing it, even

147

brought the wood for the fire). Abraham should have replied to this supposedly divine voice: "That I ought not to kill my good son is quite certain. But that you, this apparition, are God—of that I am not certain, and never can be, not even if this voice rings down to me from (visible) heaven."[43]

Kant's Copernican Revolution about authority was, in fact, exemplified by Abraham. The father of monotheism understood well that humans are the beings that follow the duty to justice and for that reason do not have the right to obey. When Kant condemns Abraham's obedience, he only translates to modern terms, as the core of Enlightenment universalism, the original Abrahamic distinction. Nothing can have authority over justice. An unjust law is no law at all. The being that is capable of following this nonhuman principle is human and commands absolute respect.

Afterword
Out of the Pit

"I FELT MY LEGS WERE PRAYING." Abraham Joshua Heschel made that remark soon after joining Martin Luther King Jr. in the third of the Selma Marches, defying along the way groups of white supremacists and police officers wielding whips, billy clubs, and tear gas. The words are almost as familiar as the black-and-white photograph of the imposing, white-bearded rabbi, flowers around his neck—the only white person in the frame with Black leaders.[1] Can we still pray with our legs?

Heschel's radicalism is familiar—his uncompromising support of the Civil Rights Movement, at times against the doubts of liberals in the center, his opposition to war, even when it was not considered the patriotic position, and his unique friendship with King. As a scholar, he was an expert of biblical prophecy: Heschel's PhD dissertation, "The Prophetic Consciousness," submitted at the University of Berlin in 1932, would be extended and published in the 1960s into *The Prophets*, a comprehensive study that became an instant classic.[2] Clearly, his research of these lost origins was not merely theoretical. Protestant German theologians in Heschel's student years used to argue that the prophets' teachings constituted the pick of Jewish development—but that Judaism in its post-prophetic era degenerated into mere national legalism. The true heir of the prophets' tradition was not Judaism but Christianity—Jesus was the heir, not the rabbis.

Heschel's theoretical work, and his life, was the refutation of that thesis. And yet this is a fact that makes his friendship with King, a Protestant minister, all the more striking. It is said that King and his associates used to carry around paperback editions of *The Prophets* and use them in speeches and sermons for inspiration.

This joint return to prophecy by the Polish Jewish refugee and scholar and the leader of the Civil Rights Movement served primarily one function: not just returning to an uncompromising idea of justice but returning to it as the sole idea that has the power to overcome nihilism. As Heschel put it,

Our world seems not unlike a pit of snakes . . . we had descended into it generations ago, and the snakes have sent their venom into the bloodstream of humanity . . . dulling our minds, darkening our vision . . . in our everyday life we worshiped force, despised compassion, and obeyed no law but our unappeasable appetite. The vision of the sacred has all but died in the soul of man. And when greed, envy and the reckless will to power, the serpents that were cherished in the bosom of our civilization, came to maturity, they broke out of their dens to fall upon the helpless nations . . . The greatest task of our time is to take the souls of men out of the pit[3].

King, of course, was facing the same task. He understood that a nihilist celebration of power and self-interest is the true enemy of justice, and that such nihilism sits deep in the minds of men. When he was dismayed by his Black allies' support of the Vietnam War, and they attacked him for opposing the war at the expense of their movement's interests, he complained of precisely that nihilism—these critics have not really "known me" or his "calling."[4] But he had one friend who certainly did understand King's "calling," not just because when he, too, opposed Vietnam he had to go against the currents in his community but because he was the author of a book titled *The Prophets*. At some point, Heschel complained, "to speak about God and remain silent on Vietnam is blasphemous." One hears an echo of that statement when King begins to speak publicly against Vietnam by breaking, as he put it, the "betrayal of my own silence."

The two walked together a long way, but in retrospect we must notice at least one topic of which they did not speak—they were both Zionists, committed to the revival of Jewish life in the post-Holocaust years, and each failed to sufficiently address Palestine. They both passed away before they had a chance to witness Israel's decades-long settlement project and the apartheid structure that's been governing the West Bank for years. They certainly did not see Hamas's brutal terrorist attack on Israeli civilians, and then Israel's systematic destruction of the possibility of a continuous Palestinian life and future in Gaza. Of course, not even these two prophets could be expected to foresee the future. But they failed to understand what could have been understood already then: that in the state of the Jews, Palestinians can hope to be at best "separate and equal," that is, second-class citizens, an idea that both men fought vehemently against in the United States. And they certainly did not appreciate the massive expulsions and dispossessions of Palestinian society as part of the past and future of the Israeli state. For all their absolute integrity, they didn't so much as see the Palestinian people.

What would they say if they were alive today? Of course, we do not know the answer, but I have no doubt about the type of answer they would give, also no doubt that they'd be speaking it out loud. It would be neither the post-Holocaust Zionist commitment to a Jewish state nor a reduction of the situation to the prism of postcolonial or critical race critique. They would have taken the position in which the commitment to the dignity of humanity, not just the justified anger or the nihilist fear of victims, takes the lead.

A friend wrote me upon reading this book as a manuscript: "For better and worse, this is a far-fetched intellectual intervention. The political questions are left open, as [are] the moral ones. What does it look like when we turn from your theoretical inquiry into the origin of universalism back to politics? You don't get your hands dirty discussing the actual identity debates; how does this defense of the humanism of Kant and the prophets look in the real world?"

The shortest example I can give by means of an answer is one I have given elsewhere at length: It looks like the Haifa Republic, the realist binational utopia I developed in my previous writings, including *Haifa Republic: A Democratic Future for Israel* (2021). The type of relation to Jewish and Palestinian identity, to speaking the truth about the Jewish and democratic contradiction to the hopes for a one-state solution in which all are equal—and a constitution opening with the unqualified premise of human dignity protects all citizens—is the type of politics for which radical universalism serves as a metaphysics.

After all, Zionism is the primary example of identity politics in the postwar era. It is also a form of identity politics that is justified, if any such politics is. The Zionist argument is the following: The universalism of the European Enlightenment has failed us. It has failed in defending our rights; it has failed in defending our culture; it most certainly failed in defending our lives. In fact, to the extent that European Fascism and Auschwitz—the sort that Heschel managed to flee but only barely —were the Enlightenment's results (think: Horkheimer and Adorno's *Dialectic of Enlightenment*), it didn't just fail in defending us but it attacked us directly, producing the death camp just as much as it produced colonialism and enslavement. Therefore, we need our own, Jewish, politics to survive.

And if you criticize that idea from a universalist perspective, this is only because as a privileged non-Jew you cannot understand Jewish experience. The thought that you have the right to judge the victims makes you anti-Semitic.

On the opposite side of this argument, we find the Palestinian people, who rightly claim they have been infiltrated and colonized by outsiders who have taken over their land, expelled them from it, and continue to oppress those remaining on it while successfully selling in the West the story of "the only democracy in the Middle East"—not to mention the current culmination of this process in Gaza's systematic eradication and the starvation of its population, while speaking of Israel's right to self-defense. The problem, one might be tempted to argue, is not that Israel is not enough of a Western liberal democracy but that this is what Western liberal democracies look like: forever built on the violent destruction of others.

Insofar as each side in this debate begins politics by the affirmation of its own identity—Jewish or Palestinian—each culminates in the erasure of the other. (And to be sure, the situation is not symmetrical: Currently, we Israelis dominate overwhelmingly in power and will be held accountable for the continuing process of ethnic cleansing and for the systematic destruction of Palestinian society, a subject I addressed in *Haifa Republic*.) To the extent, however, that we continue to argue the respective claims of, on the one hand, the Israeli "We Jews" and, on the other, "We Palestinians," each claimant will always cancel the other out—its history, legitimacy, and very existence. The reason the current debates between Zionists on the one side and postcolonialist critics on the other are so violent is not that they are different from each other but that, in their embrace of identity, they are rather similar.

Post-Holocaust Zionists resist the understanding of the Holocaust—and the creation of the State of Israel in its aftermath—as a form of colonialism because they think this relativizes the systematic extermination of European Jewry as a foundational crime. Israel is not a colonialist apartheid state, the argument goes, but the state of Holocaust survivors. Of course, this is a fallacy, for Israel can be, and unfortunately is, both. On the other side, we do find Palestinians and postcolonial critics who speak as if understanding the colonization and expulsion of Palestinians also in relation to the Holocaust is "normalization." In the terms coined by Holocaust studies, it is relativizing colonialism. At a recent conference in Berlin called "Hijacking Memory," where I was a speaker, we hoped, among other things, to problematize the systematic weaponization of the Holocaust's memory to the ongoing persecution of the Palestinians. Yet the only Palestinian speaker on the program—one of the strongest Palestinian voices in American and English circles—took the stage to deny the conference's premise: It is not that the Holocaust's memory ought not be hijacked but that it ought not be made relevant to Palestine at all. Let us be clear: This proposition is not in any way worse than the refusal to see the Jewish state as a colonizing force. But it is also not better, and it is not made better by the ability to understand the anger, even of a Palestinian.

Immediately after October 7th, Judith Butler wrote in a piece that I appreciated very much but that most people around me attacked from both left and right: "What if our morality and our politics did not end with the act of condemnation? What if we insisted on asking what form of life would release the region from violence such as this? What if, in addition to condemning wanton crimes, we wanted to create a future in which violence of this sort came to an end? That is a normative aspiration that goes beyond momentary condemnation."[5] I believe the task is exactly the one defined here by Butler: How can we imagine the first steps to the achievement of a form of life that can release the region from such violence? If I have had any criticism of Butler's expressions since, it was because I believe that they were untrue to this principle: Talking about Hamas's massacre as an act of "armed resistance" is no better than talking of Israel's destruction of the possibility of life in Gaza as an act of "self-defense" under international law. Our morality and our politics cannot *end* with the act of condemnation, but it does minimally begin by taking a clear stand. We will not take the first steps out of the current violence and so much as begin to *imagine* the possibility of cohabitation— as I do with my Palestinian friends—with those who support or tolerate Hamas's crimes against Israeli civilians, just as we will not be able to do so with those who fail to achieve clarity on Israel's crimes against Palestinians, and refuse to demand accountability for them. Cohabitation requires, at this point, the recognition that crimes must be investigated and prosecuted. That criminals must pay the price.

Immediately after the massacre, David Grossman wrote "Who

Will We Be Once We Rise from the Ashes?," in which he asked, "What do those who support the absurd notion of a binational state say today?"[6] These questions were asked in Hebrew, in the first-person plural, and to me that's the way in which it is also the most natural to ask it. But the demand to investigate and prosecute *our* war crimes, *our* criminals, already cracks the first-person "we." For that demand, recognizing the authority of law that is necessary to protect humanity, putting it before the Jewish "us," entails a recognition that the question "Who will we be?" is currently genuinely open and will not be answered only by "us." Will we agree to be a nation of war criminals, or evade that by demanding prosecution? Will we transform who we are—with Palestinian friends—beyond the insistence on Jewish sovereignty, to imagine a future beyond this violence? This is what supporters of the "absurd" idea of binationalism have to say: If a heritage of radical humanism has any future, then it will be by daring to put the answer to the question, in some sense, before the question itself. We will not be the ones giving an answer but the ones who are joined *by* the answer. The ones constituted by it. And it is an answer that too few today are willing to give, frankly on both sides—and the proof is that too many would shout "there's no symmetry" instead of giving it: That the only way to take the lives of people on either side as infinitely important is to take as equally infinitely important the lives on both sides. That therefore whatever solution there will be to this darkness it must be based not on the national sovereignty of each side but by the only principle that can be stated unconditionally: that human dignity is inviolable.

In *Haifa Republic*, I showed it is possible to think about such a radical reconstruction of the country's structure for the creation of a common concept of citizenship: A shared, binational "we" must emerge as the end of such a political process rather than the insistence of the exclusive identitarian "we" in the beginning.

The commitment to such an ideal of humanity doesn't erase identities; to the contrary, it is identities that cancel each other out. Ultimately, only universalism will defend them. Fake universalism will not do that, only the true, radical kind. And to achieve it, as Heschel and King knew, is not easy and would require getting the minds of people out of the pit.

Appendix: The Opposite of Forgetting

The text below was written as the keynote address for the official ceremony in which Germany commemorated eighty years since the liberation of the Buchenwald Concentration Camp. After intense pressure by the Israeli embassy in Berlin, the speech was canceled. Its publication by the German daily Süddeutsche Zeitung *on the eve of the ceremony ignited intense public debate on the meaning of the term* nie wieder—*never again—and Germany's commitment to Israel, international law, and universal principles amid the war in Gaza.*

Yosef Hayim Yerushalmi (1922–2009), the towering historian of Jewish memory, ended his classic volume, *Zakhor: Jewish History and Jewish Memory*,[1] with a question: "What if the antonym of 'forgetting' isn't 'remembering', but 'justice'?" Yerushalmi himself never answered the question or even bothered to explain what he meant. But it provides the cue to thinking of memory—its significance, its authority—in days that present new and unbearable challenges to keeping it intact.

According to Yerushalmi, there is in the Jewish tradition a sharp distinction between history and memory. Whereas history is written in the third person—making a claim to factual knowledge over the past—memory can only be told in the first person, whether singular or plural. Memory is neither merely factual nor descriptive; it always makes a claim upon us—a call for action, a duty. Here lies the deepest difference between history and memory: Whereas history truly is about the past, memory turns out to be focused on the future. And it is for this reason that it is possible to remember and still forget: The opposite of forgetting isn't just knowing the past but remaining committed to the duty that stands before us.

This realization helps in resolving an apparent contradiction that could seem to lie at the heart of Jewish cultural life. On the one hand, Judaism is famously occupied with memory. On the other, it is a prophetic tradition, predominantly interested in the future—even with the utopian or the ideal. But the tension is only artificial: When the prophets call upon us again and again to *Remember! Zakhor!*, they demand that we never forget, that only doing justice in the future is doing justice to the past.

I want to argue that this position, interpreted out of Yerushalmi, is in fact incomplete. For the ideal that the prophets taught us to seek is not in the final analysis justice, but peace. Martin Buber is remembered as a thinker who understood that clearly. But Hermann Cohen was the one who articulated it most forcefully, explaining that justice is not the highest moral end because it depends on judgment and as such on incompleteness, or separation. In the Jewish tradition, he says, peace is superior to justice, occupying an analogous position to that of harmony in the Greek conception: it is the perfect, the whole. *Shalem* in Hebrew means "whole," and it gives the origin to shalom, "peace," which complements justice by universalizing it, becoming "the epitome of human life in the Bible" and serves as "the highest archetype of human morality."[2]

Of course, Cohen sees in front of his eyes not just the prophets but a combination of the prophets and Immanuel Kant's Enlightenment, which culminated with the ideal he envisioned in "Perpetual Peace." Against the doctrine of Heraclitus, convincing to supporters of "realist" politics, according to which "war is the father of all things," the Hebrew prophets and Kant posed a radical alternative. Not the alleged reality and necessity of war but the ideal of peace must stand as the origin of human relations, human politics, human law.

Of course, Kant knew just as well as the prophets before him that in our violent world reality is far from a utopian vision. But this was just the point: He observed, correctly, that amid the brutal—he said "barbaric"—reality, we must hold ourselves accountable to the authority of the laws of this ideal's *possibility*. He warned that short of remaining true to this ideal of peace, humanity would eventually inevitably slide into full destruction through wars of extermination. When we remember Buchenwald's horrors, when we look again at the unbearable images that were taken when the camp was liberated by American troops, and as we look in the eyes of the survivors who are still with us—some of them were in these very pictures—I cannot but help thinking of that Kantian warning, in line with the prophets, as the correction to Yerushalmi's question. Can it be that the opposite of forgetting is neither remembering nor justice, but peace?

And let us be clear, there are other, competing Jewish traditions of memory, not all of them the ones I articulated. The most significant alternative begins with a statement that has recently become too familiar: "Remember [*zakhor*] that which was done to you by Amalek"[3] and "eradicate its seed."[4] Both of these traditions of memory are open before us. Which one will we choose? At what consequences?

"Perpetual Peace" was published in 1795 and seemed in Kant's day entirely utopian. "Good in theory but not in practice," as the familiar saying of "realist" opponents went even back then.

Yet its underlying principles were incorporated into international law after World War II as a response to the destruction and the images that came out of camps like the one that we are gathered here to commemorate. In the images that came out of Buchenwald—and out of Auschwitz, Treblinka, Sobibor, and so many other places—humanity looked in the mirror and discovered that it has been engaged in more than just unlimited war and mass murder, but through the rabid anti-Semitism that led to the systematic attempt to eradicate the Jews from the face of the earth, an attack on the very idea of human dignity.

The idea of dignity had been familiar for some time; it was from these images that its urgent significance as a condition of our shared life on earth was discovered, and for the first time—this is often overlooked—was incorporated into state constitutions and international conventions. The achievements of documents like the United Nations Universal Declaration of Human Rights or German Basic Law lie in understanding that the rule of law and international law are themselves grounded in moral commitments. From the horrors confronted in a place like Buchenwald, a previously utopian-looking thought became an actual process that attempted to protect all humans not just as citizens, by their states, but also from their states and by all means if they are—like the Jews in Buchenwald—not citizens at all. Through the incorporation of the ideal of dignity into law, humanity refused to let war—the ultimate contradiction of any ideal—be the father of all things. And it chose instead to inscribe *nie wieder*, *never again*, into human existence—this deepest articulation of our duties to the future through the commitment to the past—by deriving our commitment to laws from the ideals of dignity and peace.

It is sometimes claimed that this statement, *never again*, admits of two formulations. One is simply *never again*. The other is, in view of the genocidal anti-Semitism that culminated in the Final Solution, *never again to us*: The task can be allegedly seen as limited to ensuring that Jews never face extermination. It is time to put this distinction aside. *Never again* is only valid in its universal form, among other things because only in its universal form can it do justice to its particular formulation. A world in which a repetition of the horrors that we have seen here is a world in which wars of extermination are possible everywhere, by all means also against Jews. Only an international community that pledges to eradicate the possibility of unlimited wars is one that ensures that the same crimes would never reoccur.

People sometimes speak of October 7th saying *never again*; meanwhile others look at Gaza and say the same thing. Insofar as either of these is intended as a comparison to the Holocaust —each side and its own relativization—the one is as misleading as the other. But both statements also have a kernel of truth in them, in that both expose the failure to prevent the complete dehumanization of enemies and societies and that both expose an international community—each and the side it supports—that has been willing to tolerate, sometimes to justify, dehumanizing crimes that subvert the very possibility of peace.

It is not too dramatic to say that, as we mark the liberation of the camp eighty years ago, the world is now coming into a new epoch. The United States, which liberated this camp—marking the beginning of a long-standing American-European alliance that stands for liberal democracy—is starting to turn its back on its liberal allies, just as much as it is on the rule of law and international law. Putin is advancing an unlimited war of aggression on Ukraine, and the European Union enters an entirely new phase in which it will have to take its protection into its own hands, becoming a military power. As these transformations take shape, European nationalist populists are on the rise, enjoying alliances in the United States and elsewhere. Such European nationalists become the most dangerous not when they pretend to disown their Fascist and anti-Semitic origins but when they claim to be—through their opposition to the rule of law, international law, to Europe and its Enlightenment—the actual bearers of responsibility for the past.

Let us warn against them loudly, but meanwhile not forget to check ourselves. To make sure that as the democratic right, the democratic center, and the democratic left fight against nationalists, we still remain the alternative, one that stands by the genuine commitment to the rule of law and international law. One that still knows *why* these notions are necessary to protect the ideal of human dignity and resists the temptation posed by the alleged realist doctrines, which ask to build European power with diminished commitments to the rule of law. Such realist doctrines will quickly bring us from *never again* back to *again*. There is nothing realist in overlooking the inevitable wars of extermination that the ideals of dignity and peace were meant to preclude. To oppose these trends, it is necessary to remember Buchenwald, but it is not enough. We also make sure that we never forget.

Notes

INTRODUCTION

1. W. E. B. Du Bois, *Black Reconstruction in America: An Essay Toward a History of the Part Which Black Folk Played in the Attempt to Reconstruct Democracy in America, 1860–1880* (Harcourt, Brace and Co., 1935).

2. See W. E. B. Du Bois, *Dusk of Dawn: An Essay Toward and Autobiography of a Race Concept* (Oxford University Press, 2007).

3. W. E. B. Du Bois, "Acceptance speech by Dr. W. E. B. Du Bois, June 23, 1960." James Aronson–W. E. B. Du Bois Collection (MS 292). Special Collections and University Archives, University of Massachusetts Amherst Libraries, https://credo.library.umass.edu/view/full/mums292-b001-i142.

4. Michael Steinberg speaking at Cornell University, https://www.cornell.edu/video/michael-p-steinberg-martin-luther-king-jr-east-west-berlin.

5. Jan-Werner Mueller, "The Fairy Tale of the Illiberal Left," *IPS* (August 21, 2020): https://www.ips-journal.eu/topics/democracy/the-fairy-tale-of-the-illiberal-left-4584/.

6. Ibid.

7. See Robert Bernasconi, "Kant as an Unfamiliar Source of Racism," in *Philosophers on Race: Critical Essays*, edited by Julie K. Ward and Tommy L. Lott (Blackwell Publishers, 2002), 145–66; but especially Charles Mills, *The Racial Contract* (Cornell University Press, 1997), 72.

8. Samuel Moyn, "The Modernization of Duties," *Liberties* 2:2 (2022): 52. It is remarkable that this powerful essay refrains from mentioning the one modern philosopher who did strive to modernize the concept of duty, namely Immanuel Kant. Arguably, this isn't a side episode in the development of modern political thinking. For a notable exception, see Aleida Assmann, *Menschenrechte und Menschenpflichten: Schlüsselbegriffe für eine humane Gesellschaft* (Picus Verlag, 2018).

9. Robert Cover, "Obligation: A Jewish Jurisprudence of the Social Order," *Journal of Law and Religion* 5:1 (1987): 65–74.

10. Richard Rorty, *Achieving Our Country: Leftist Thought in Twentieth-Century America* (Harvard University Press, 1998).

11. Mark Lilla, *The Once and Future Liberal: After Identity Politics* (Harper, 2017).

12. Jill Lepore, *This America: The Case for the Nation* (Liveright Publishing Corporation, 2019), 20.

13. Anthony Appiah: "The Uncompleted Argument: Du Bois and the Illusion of Race," in *"Race," Writing, and Difference*, edited by Henry Louis Gates Jr. (University of Chicago Press, 1985). See also Bernasconi, "Kant as an Unfamiliar Source of Racism," and Stuart Hall, *The Fateful Triangle: Race, Ethnicity, Nation* (Harvard University Press, 2017).

14. Immanuel Kant, "An Answer to the Question: What Is Enlighten-

ment?," translated by James Schmidt, in *What Is Enlightenment?: Eighteenth-Century Answers and Twentieth-Century Questions*, translated by James Schmidt et al., edited by James Schmidt (University of California Press, 1996), 58.

15. See Rorty, *Achieving Our Country*, 18, where the idea is ascribed to Dewey and Whitman. See also his *Pragmatism as Anti-Authoritarianism* (The Belknap Press of Harvard University Press, 2021), 126–43.

16. Friedrich Nietzsche, *The Gay Science*, translated by Josefine Nauckhoff and Adrian Del Caro (Cambridge University Press, 2001).

17. Sigmund Freud, *Moses and Monotheism*, translated by Katherine Jones (Vintage Books, 1967).

18. Jan Assmann, *The Price of Monotheism*, translated by Robert Savage (Stanford University Press, 2010).

19. Richard Rorty, "Pragmatism as Romantic Polytheism," in *Philosophy as Cultural Politics: Philosophical Papers*, vol. 4 (Cambridge, 2007), 27–41.

20. Genesis 18:25.

THE MARK OF CAIN

1. See for example W. E. B. Du Bois, *John Brown*, edited by Henry Louis Gates Jr. (Oxford University Press, 2007), 152–54; Tony Horwitz, *Midnight Rising: John Brown and the Raid That Sparked the Civil War* (Henry Holt and Company, 2011), 5. The first philosophical account in modern history of John Brown as a philosophical problem, and indeed grasping Brown as a hero rather than a madman, was given by Susan Neiman's Tanner Lectures on Human Values, delivered at the University of Michigan, March 26, 2010.

2. See Mr. Vallandigham in the *Cincinnati Enquirer*; cited in Henry D. Thoreau, "A Plea for Captain John Brown," in *Essays*, edited by Jeffery S. Cramer (Yale University Press, 2013), 206; Charles J. G. Griffin, "John Brown's 'Madness,'" *Rhetoric & Public Affairs* 12:3 (2009): 370.

3. Abolitionist editor William Lloyd Garrison; cited in Griffin, "John Brown's 'Madness,'" 370.

4. Abraham Lincoln, Speech at Leavenworth, Kansas, December 3, 1859, in *Collected Works of Abraham Lincoln*, vol. 3 (Rutgers University Press, 1953), 502.

5. Du Bois, *John Brown*, 15.

6. William Lloyd Garrison in his newspaper *The Liberator*; cited in Louis Menand, *The Metaphysical Club: A Story of Ideas in America* (Farrar, Straus and Giroux, 2001), 14; based on Isaiah 28:15.

7. Ralph Waldo Emerson, lecture in Tremont Temple for the Parker Fraternity, "Courage," Boston, November 8, 1859; cited in George Willis Cooke, *Ralph Waldo Emerson: His Life, Writings, and Philosophy* (James R. Osgood and Company, 1882), 140.

8. Thoreau, "A Plea for Captain John Brown," 204.

9. Alexis de Tocqueville, "The Majority in the United States Is All-Powerful and the Consequences of That," in *Democracy in America*, vol. 1, in *Democracy and Two Essays on America*, translated by Gerald E. Bevan (Penguin, 2003).

10. Thoreau, "A Plea for Captain John Brown," 213.

11. Ibid., 204.

12. Ibid., 201.

13. Ralph Waldo Emerson to Oliver Wendell Holmes, March 1856, in *The Selected Letters of Ralph Waldo Emerson*, edited by Joel Myerson (Columbia University Press, 1997), 389.

14. William Ellery Channing, "Remarks on Associations" (1829), in *Works of William Ellery Channing, D. D.* (J. Munroe, 1841–1843), vol. 1, 290; cited in Menand, *The Metaphysical Club*, 19–20.

15. Ralph Waldo Emerson, "Self-Reliance," in *The Essential Writings of Ralph Waldo Emerson*, edited by Brooks Atkinson (The Modern Library, 2000), 132. The relation between Emerson and Tocqueville isn't always noticed. Interestingly enough, Emerson knew Tocqueville's thesis through John Mill's review of *Democracy in America*, and then an approving discussion of the tyranny of the masses thesis.

16. Victor Hugo to the editor of *London News*, December 2, 1859, in *The Tribunal: Responses to John Brown and the Harpers Ferry Raid*, edited by John Stauffer and Zoe Trodd (The Belknap Press of Harvard University Press, 2012), 371.

17. John Locke, *Second Treatise on Government*, in *Two Treatises of Government*, edited by Peter Laslett (Cambridge University Press, 2003), 265–428. For the sources of the draft of the Declaration, see Carl L. Becker, *The Declaration of Independence: A Study in the History of Political Ideas* (Harcourt, Brace and Company, 1922).

18. Leo Strauss notices the problem in his introduction to *Natural Right and History* (University of Chicago Press, 1965), 1–8, and his students are among the few who addressed the problem directly. See Harry Jaffa, *Crisis of the House Divided: An Interpretation of the Issues in the Lincoln-Douglas Debates* (University of Chicago Press, 2009) and *A New Birth of Freedom: Abraham Lincoln and the Coming of the Civil War* (Rowman & Littlefield Publishing Group, 2018). However, these treatments serve Straussians to justify a return—arguably reactionary—to ancient philosophy, in particular Aristotle, in answering nihilism, or what they call the "crisis of modernity," instead of seeking a modern

answer to the impact of natural science on natural law. In the process, they conveniently ignore Kant, the one philosopher who grasped the same problem and attempted a modern answer. Strauss himself, in *Natural Right and History*, analyzes the crisis of modernity by going over Weber (together with his discussion of "historicism" probably a code name for Heidegger [!]), Hobbes, Locke, Machiavelli, and Burke, concluding with a discussion of Rousseau's (for Strauss ultimately unsuccessful) attempt to resolve it. Kant remains unmentioned.

19. Friedrich Nietzsche, "The Birth of Tragedy," in *The Birth of Tragedy: And Other Writings*, translated by Ronald Speirs, edited by Raymond Geuss and Ronald Speirs (Cambridge University Press, 1999), 9.

20. Friedrich Nietzsche, "On Truth and Lie in an Extra-Moral Sense (1873)," in *Writings from the Early Notebooks*, translated by Ladislaus Löb, edited by Raymond Geuss and Alexander Nehamas (Cambridge University Press, 2009), 253.

21. Jeremy Waldron, *God, Locke, and Equality: Christian Foundations in Locke's Political Thought* (Cambridge University Press, 2002).

22. Jürgen Habermas, "The Controversy over the Secularization Hypothesis and the Role of Religion in a Post-Secular Society," Yale University, October 6, 2008; "The Secular Level of Intercultural Communication in an Emergent, Multicultural World Society," Yale University, October 7, 2008; "On the Self-Understanding of Secular Reason," October 13, 2008, Yale University.

23. Jürgen Habermas, *Postmetaphysical Thinking: Philosophical Essays* (MIT Press, 1992), 51. Peter Gordon and Jay Bernstein launch a critique of Habermas: see Peter E. Gordon, *Migrants in the Profane: Critical Theory and the Question of Secularization* (Yale University Press, 2020); "Critical Theory Between the Sacred and the Profane,"

Constellations 23:4 (2016): 466–81; "Kritische Theorie zwischen Sakralen und Profane," *WestEnd: Neue Zeitschrift für Sozialforschung* 1 (2016): 3–34; and J. M. Bernstein, *Recovering Ethical Life: Jürgen Habermas and the Future of Critical Theory* (Routledge, 1995).

24. It is sometimes overlooked that Jacobi first used the term only in 1799, referring to Johanne Gottlieb Fichte's position; see Jacobi's "Brief an Fichte," in *Appellation an das Publikum ... Dokumente zum Atheismusstreit um Fichte, Forberg und Niethammer* (Reclam, 1987), 153–67. But Jacobi's conclusion that Enlightenment leads to Spinozism (and hence pantheism, fatalism, and atheism) is the origin of his term "nihilism."

25. See Steven Nadler's description in *A Book Forged in Hell: Spinoza's Scandalous Treatise and the Birth of the Secular Age* (Princeton University Press, 2011).

26. Jonathan Israel has proven this fact beyond doubt in his monumental trilogy on the radical Enlightenment; see *Radical Enlightenment: Philosophy and the Making of Modernity 1650–1750*; *Enlightenment Contested: Philosophy, Modernity, and the Emancipation of Man 1670–1752*; and *Democratic Enlightenment: Philosophy, Revolution, and Human Rights 1750–1790*. One needn't agree with everything that Israel says, or his interpretation of Spinoza's philosophy, to recognize the unmistakable impact of Spinoza's philosophy, which was previously unrecognized. Works like Pierre Bayle's *Dictonnaire*, Denis Diderot and Jean le Rond d'Alembert's *Encyclopédie*, and Johann Heinrich Zedler's *Lexikon* devote significantly more attention to it than to Locke, Hobbes, Plato, or Aristotle. Spinoza's philosophy was not ignored, and it could not be. See my review of Israel's trio in *Notre Dame Philosophical Review* (February 6, 2012), https://ndpr.nd.edu

/reviews/democratic-enlightenment-philosophy-revolution-and-human-rights-1750-1790/.

27. Benedict de Spinoza, *Ethics*, vol. 1 of *Spinoza: The Collected Works*, translated and edited by Edwin Curley (Princeton University Press, 1985), part 3, prop. 9, scholium.

28. Ibid., part 4, prop. 68, scholium.

29. Job 38:1–4.

30. See Cohen's attack on Spinoza's betrayal of Judaism in *Spinoza on State & Religion, Judaism & Christianity*, translated by Robert S. Schine (Shalem Press, 2014).

31. Friedrich Nietzsche to Franz Overbeck, July 30, 1881, in *The Portable Nietzsche*, translated and edited by Walter Kaufmann (Penguin Books, 1982), 92.

32. Immanuel Kant, *Critique of Pure Reason*, translated by Norman Kemp Smith (Palgrave Macmillan, 2007), 29, Bxxx.

33. Immanuel Kant, *Critique of Practical Reason*, translated by Mary Gregor (Cambridge University Press, 2015), 82.

34. Ibid.

35. Ibid., 83.

36. Ibid., 82.

37. Kant, *Critique of Pure Reason*, 7.

38. Ibid.

39. Nietzsche, "On Truth and Lie in an Extra-Moral Sense," in *The Portable Nietzsche*, 46.

40. Theodor Adorno and Max Horkheimer set the tone when they repeatedly complained that Enlightenment never circumscribed its "instrumental" and "positivist" concept of knowledge. Since they cannot ignore the little fact that *Critique of Pure Reason* poses an exception,

they add dismissively, "where it restricted knowledge, it generally did so to make room for faith"; see Max Horkheimer and Theodor W. Adorno, *Dialectic of Enlightenment: Philosophical Fragments*, translated by Edmund Jephcott, edited by Gunzelin Schmid Noerr (Stanford University Press, 2002), 14. This failure to take Kant's restriction of knowledge and account of faith seriously leads to their gross misreading of Kant as a positivist, too. But whereas Adorno and Horkheimer's analysis of the dialectic of Enlightenment is exactly right, their inability to see that Kant is already responding to that dialectic is striking. Jonathan Israel repeats the same idea when he characterizes Kant as a "moderate" thinker as opposed to the "radical" enlightenment of Spinoza; see Israel, *Democratic Enlightenment*, 729.

41. Immanuel Kant, "An Answer to the Question: What Is Enlightenment?," translated by James Schmidt, in *What Is Enlightenment?: Eighteenth-Century Answers and Twentieth-Century Questions*, translated by James Schmidt et al., edited by James Schmidt (University of California Press, 1996), 58.

42. As Ernst Cassirer showed, Kant took the original insight from Rousseau; see Ernst Cassirer, *The Question of Jean-Jacques Rousseau*, translated and edited by Peter Gay (Yale University Press, 1989).

43. Immanuel Kant, *Groundwork of the Metaphysics of Morals*, translated and edited by Mary Gregor (Cambridge University Press, 2006), 42.

44. This type of faith is similar to the Cartesian proof in the third Meditation, where Descartes recognizes an idea of infinity of which he himself could not have been the origin; see René Descartes, *Meditations on First Philosophy*, in *The Philosophical Writings of René Descartes*, translated and edited by John Cottingham, Robert Stoothoff, and Dugald Murdoch (Cambridge University Press, 1985), vol. 2, 31–36;

Oeuvres de Descartes, edited by Charles Adam and Paul Tannery (Librairie Philosophique J. Vrin, 1964), vol. 7, 45–52. Kant famously refutes this type of argument as an ontological argument; but he ends up accepting the same structure as a basis of proof, based on moral rather than theoretical considerations: The *absolute* demand of justice could not have come either from us or, indeed, from nature, which is blind; see *Critique of Pure Reason*, 500–7.

45. Immanuel Kant, "On the Miscarriage of All Philosophical Trials in Theodicy," in *Religion and Rational Theology*, translated and edited by Allen W. Wood and George di Giovanni (Cambridge University Press, 2001), 33.
46. Job 42:7–8.
47. Genesis 18:23–25.
48. Job 9:4.
49. Job 9:22–23.
50. The similarities between both texts are numerous. I go over them in "'He Destroys Both the Innocent with the Wicked': Between Job and Abraham," chapter 8 of *The Binding of Isaac: A Religious Model of Disobedience* (Continuum, 2007), 86–100.
51. Genesis 18:18–19.
52. Genesis 22.
53. Immanuel Kant, *The Conflict of the Faculties*, translated by Mary J. Gregor (Orbis, 1979), 115.
54. Heinrich Heine, *On the History of Religion and Philosophy in Germany*, translated by Howard Pollack-Milgate, edited by Terry Pinkard (Cambridge University Press, 2007), 78–79.
55. *Critique of Pure Reason*, 310.

56. Danielle Allen is suggesting a similar view of that sentence as a syllogism in *Our Declaration: A Reading of the Declaration of Independence in Defense of Equality* (W. W. Norton & Company, 2014). But she offers a very different account of the grounds of the premise—where the self-evident truths are allegedly empirically self-evident.

57. Cited in Jaffa, *Crisis of the House Divided*, 313–14.

58. Ibid., 314.

59. Cited in Jaffa, *A New Birth of Freedom*, 406.

60. Ibid., 292.

61. The text is reproduced in Becker, *The Declaration of Independence.*

62. Immanuel Kant, *Physische Geographie*, edited by Friedrich Theodor Rink and Paul Gedan in vol. 9 of *Werke*, 316.

63. Charles W. Mills, *The Racial Contract* (Cornell University Press, 1997), 72.

64. Immanuel Kant, "Remarks in the *Observations on the Feeling of the Beautiful and Sublime* (1764–65)," translated by Thomas Hilgers, Uygar Abacı, Michael Nance, and Paul Guyer, in *Observations on the Feeling of the Beautiful and Sublime and Other Writings*, edited by Patrick Frierson and Paul Guyer (Cambridge University Press, 2011), 125. See Karl Ameriks for an important account: "The Fate of Dignity: How Words Matter," in *Kant's Concept of Dignity*, edited by Yasushi Kato and Gerhard Schönrich, vol. 209 of *Kantstudien-Ergänzungshefte* (De Gruyter, 2020), 261–82.

65. Kant, *AA*, vol. 8, 99–100.

66. See Immanuel Kant, "Toward Perpetual Peace (1795)," in *Practical Philosophy*, translated and edited by Mary Gregor (Cambridge University Press, 1996), 325–31; "Zum ewigen Frieden: Ein philoso-

phischer Entwurf," 354–60.

67. Kant, *Groundwork of the Metaphysics of Morals*, 490.

68. Martin Luther King Jr., *Letter from Birmingham Jail* (Penguin Books, 2018), 3.

69. The White Ministers' Good Friday Statement, April 12, 1963, Appendix 2, in S. Jonathan Bass, *Blessed Are the Peacemakers: Martin Luther King Jr., Eight White Religious Leaders, and the "Letter from Birmingham Jail"* (University of Tennessee Press, 1996), 235–36.

70. The White Ministers' Law and Order Statement, January 16, 1963, "An Appeal for Law and Order and Common Sense," Appendix 1, in Bass, *Blessed Are the Peacemakers*, 233–34.

71. Ibid., 235.

72. King, *Letter from Birmingham Jail*, 1.

73. Ibid., 1.

74. Ibid., 7.

75. Ibid.,9.

76. Ibid., 7; St. Augustine, *On Free Choice of the Will*, translated by Thomas Williams (Hackett, 1993), book 1, chapter 5.

77. Ibid., 8; St. Thomas Aquinas, *Summa Theologiæ*, part 1.2ae, questions 90–108.

78. Ibid., 5.

79. Martin Luther King Jr., "Beyond Vietnam: A Time to Break Silence," speech delivered on April 4, 1967, in *The Radical King*, edited by Cornel West (Beacon Press, 2015), 202.

80. Cited in James Forman, *The Making of Black Revolutionaries* (University of Washington Press, 1997), 369.

81. Michael Eric Dyson, *I May Not Get There with You: The True Martin Luther King, Jr.* (The Free Press, 2000), 55.

TRUTH, ENEMY OF THE PEOPLE

1. See Harry G. Frankfurt, *On Bullshit* (Princeton University Press, 2005).

2. Michael M. Grynbaum, "Trump Strategist Stephen Bannon Says Media Should 'Keep Its Mouth Shut,'" *The New York Times* (online), January 26, 2017.

3. William P. Davis, "'Enemy of the People': Trump Breaks Out This Phrase During Moments of Peak Criticism," *The New York Times* (online), July 19, 2018.

4. "Fact Check: President Biden's Address to Congress," NPR, updated April 28, 2021, https://www.npr.org/2021/04/28/989120226/bidens-address-to-congress-annotated.

5. The Public Editor, "When to Call a Lie a Lie," *The New York Times*, September 20, 2016, https://www.nytimes.com/2016/09/20/public-editor/trump-birther-lie-liz-spayd-public-editor.html.

6. See Richard Rorty, *Take Care of Freedom and Truth Will Take Care of Itself: Interviews with Richard Rorty*, edited by Eduardo Mendieta (Stanford University Press, 2006).

7. Thomas Jefferson, *Notes on the State of Virginia*, 1784, query XVII.

8. Richard Rorty, "The Priority of Democracy to Philosophy," in *Objectivity, Relativism, and Truth*, vol. 1 of *Philosophical Papers* (Cambridge University Press, 1991), 175–96.

9. Richard Rorty, *Achieving Our Country: Leftist Thought in Twentieth-Century America* (Harvard University Press, 1998), 18.

10. Ludwig Wittgenstein, *Tractatus Logico-Philosphicus*, translated by D. F. Pears and B. F. McGuinness (Routledge & Kegan Paul, 1974), 1.1, 6.41.

11. Ibid., 6.42, 6.4, 6.421.

12. Quoted in "Nazi Philosophy and Truth," *Nature* 134 (October 1934): 564–65.

13. This is, for example, the line advanced in *The 1619 Project: A New Origin Story*, created by Nikole Hannah-Jones and *The New York Times Magazine* (One-World, 2021).

14. W. E. B. Du Bois, *Black Reconstruction: An Essay Toward a History of the Part Which Black Folk Played in the Attempt to Reconstruct Democracy in America, 1860–1880* (Harcourt, Brace and Company, 1935), 716.

15. Ibid., 716.

16. Cited in Franny Nudelman, *John Brown's Body: Slavery, Violence, and the Culture of War* (University of North Carolina Press, 2004), 14–15.

17. Abraham Lincoln, "Address at Gettysburg, November 19th, 1863," in *1863–1865*, vol. 7 of *The Writings of Abraham Lincoln*, edited by Arthur Brooks Lapsley (P. F. Collier & Son Publishers, 1865), 21–22.

18. Jonathan Lear, "Gettysburg Mourning," *Critical Inquiry* 45:1 (2018): 97–121, 104.

19. Ibid., 109.

20. Ibid., 109, 115–16.

21. Lincoln, "Address at Gettysburg," 24.

22. Oliver Wendell Holmes Jr., "Notes on Albert Durer," *The Harvard Magazine* 7:58 (1861): 41–77, 43.

23. Oliver Wendell Holmes Jr., "Books," *The Harvard Magazine* 4:10 (1858): 408–12, 410. Emphasis mine.

24. Ralph Waldo Emerson, "Attempted Speech: 24 January 1861," *Emerson's Antislavery Writings*, edited by Len Gougeon and Joel Myerson (Yale University Press, 1995), 127; cited in Louis Menand, *The Meta-*

physical Club: A Story of Ideas in America (Farrar, Straus and Giroux, 2001), 31.

25. Oliver Wendell Holmes Jr. to Harold J. Laski, May 12, 1927, in *1926–1935*, vol. 2 of *Holmes-Laski Letters: The Correspondence of Mr. Justice Holmes and Harold J. Laski, 1916–1935*, edited by Mark DeWolfe Howe (Harvard University Press), 942; cited in Menand, *The Metaphysical Club*, 62.

26. Holmes to Laski, June 1, 1927, in ibid., 948; cited in Menand, *The Metaphysical Club*, 63.

27. Holmes to Laski, September 15, 1929, in ibid., 1183.

28. Ralph Waldo Emerson, "Self-Reliance," in *The Essential Writings of Ralph Waldo Emerson*, edited by Brooks Atkinson (The Modern Library, 2000), 132.

29. Oliver Wendell Holmes Jr., "The Gas-Stokers' Strike," *American Law Review* 7:3 (1873), 583.

30. Oliver Wendell Holmes Jr., *The Common Law* (The Belknap Press of Harvard University Press, 2009), 42, 4.

31. Ibid., 3.

32. Oliver Wendell Holmes Jr., "Natural Law," in *The Fundamental Holmes: A Free Speech Chronicle and Reader*, edited by Ronald K. L. Collins (Cambridge University Press, 2010), 201. Emphasis mine

33. Benedict de Spinoza, *Ethics*, in vol. 1 of *Spinoza: The Collected Works*, translated and edited by Edwin Curley (Princeton University Press, 1985), part 3, prop. 9, scholium.

34. Richard A. Posner, *The Problems of Jurisprudence* (Harvard University Press, 1993), 240.

35. Holmes, "Natural Law," 201.

36. Friedrich Nietzsche, "On Truth and Lie in an Extra-Moral Sense (1873)," in *Writings from the Early Notebooks*, translated by Ladislaus Löb, edited by Raymond Geuss and Alexander Nehamas (Cambridge University Press, 2009), 253.

37. Holmes, "Natural Law," 199.

38. John Dewey, "The Future of Liberalism," in *1935–1937*, vol. 11 of *The Later Works, 1915–1953*, part 3 of *The Collected Works of John Dewey*, edited by Jo Ann Boydston (Southern Illinois University Press, 2008), 291.

39. Holmes, *The Common Law*, 3–4.

40. Oliver Wendell Holmes Jr. to Sir Frederick Pollock, May 15, 1931, in *Holmes-Pollock Letters: The Correspondence of Mr. Justice Holmes and Sir Frederick Pollock, 1874–1932* (Harvard University Press, 1942), vol. 2, 287; cited in Menand, *The Metaphysical Club*, 437.

41. John Dewey, *German Philosophy and Politics* (Henry Holt and Company, 1915), 89.

42. Ibid., 51.

43. Richard Rorty, "Pragmatism as Romantic Polytheism," in *Philosophy as Cultural Politics: Philosophical Papers*, vol. 4 (Cambridge University Press, 2007), 39.

44. Sidney Hook, *Education and the Taming of Power* (Open Court Publishing Company, 1973), 141.

45. Martin Luther King Jr., *Letter from Birmingham Jail* (Penguin Books, 2018), 27.

46. Du Bois, *Black Reconstruction*, 726.

47. Rorty, *Achieving Our Country*, 90.

48. Mark Lilla, "The End of Identity Liberalism," November 18, 2016,

The New York Times, https://www.nytimes.com/2016/11/20/opinion /sunday/the-end-of-identity-liberalism.html; and *The Once and Future Liberal: After Identity Politics* (HarperCollins, 2018).

49. Lilla, *The Once and Future Liberal*, 7–8.

50. Ibid., 8.

51. Ibid.

52. Ibid., 32, 117.

53. Ibid., 102, 101, 59.

54. See Randy Kennedy, "White Artist's Painting of Emmett Till at Whitney Biennial Draws Protests," *The New York Times*, March 21, 2017.

55. "'What a Mother Should Tell Her Child': Mother's Day Sermon at Ebenezer Baptist Church," in: Martin Luther King Jr. Papers, 1950–1968, Martin Luther King Jr., Center for Nonviolent Social Change, Inc., Atlanta, 12.5. 1963.

56. Hannah Black, open letter to the curators and staff of the Whitney Biennial; cited in Alex Greenberger, "'The Painting Must Go': Hannah Black Pens Open Letter to the Whitney About Controversial Biennial Work," in *ARTnews* (March 21, 2017), https://www.artnews.com/ artnews/news/the-painting-must-go-hannah-black-pens-open-letter-to-the-whitney-about-controversial-biennial-work-7992/.

57. Richter used for the paintings four photographs that were taken by inmates inside the gas chambers and smuggled out of Auschwitz. In one of the photos, bodies are seen lying outside of the chambers, waiting to be burned at the crematorium. In another, prisoners are seen dragging inmates' bodies into the fire. A third picture presents naked women in a forest, on their way to be gassed; the last one shows only a branch and some sky. As far as we know, these are the only

photographs smuggled out of the camps by inmates. Richter reproduced them in enlarged measures, painted over them abstractly with brown, gray, and black, accompanied by touches of green and red. It is impossible to recognize the original photos under the painting's abstraction.

58. Dana Schutz, emailed statement; cited in Oliver Basciano, "Whitney Biennial: Emmet Till Casket Painting by White Artist Sparks Anger," *The Guardian*, March 21, 2017, https://www.theguardian.com/artanddesign/2017/mar/21/whitney-biennial-emmett-till-painting-dana-schutz.

59. I analyzed at length the use and abuse of Holocaust commemoration, once it is carried out from such a perspective, in *Haifa Republic* (NYRB, 2021). See "Remembering and Forgetting: The Holocaust".

60. Roland Barthes, "The Death of the Author," in *Image Music Text*, translated by Stephen Heath (Fontana Press, 1977), 142–48.

61. Ibid., 143.

62. Theodor W. Adorno, *Kant's Critique of Pure Reason*, translated by Rodney Livingstone, edited by Rolf Tiedemann (Stanford University Press, 2001), 63.

63. Barthes, "The Death of the Author," 142.

64. Barthes would have been surprised to find himself in the same boat as Kant; but then, as Kant once said, "we often understand an [author] better than he has understood himself." See Immanuel Kant, *Critique of Practical Reason*, translated by Mary Gregor (Cambridge University Press, 2015), 310.

65. Rorty, "The Priority of Democracy to Philosophy," 176.

66. Lilla, *The Once and Future Liberal*, 14.

67. Ibid., 120.

68. Ibid., 137.

69. Ibid., 120.

70. The aim of my *Haifa Republic* (New York Review Books, 2021) is to offer a model for such a revision of Israel's civic identity—proposing the revisions of memory, legislation, and self-understanding beginning with the duty to humans rather than with Jewish identity.

71. Lilla, *The Once and Future Liberal*, 15n.

72. John Rawls, "Justice as Fairness: Political not Metaphysical," in *Collected Papers*, edited by Samuel Freeman (Harvard University Press, 1999), 388–414.

73. Ibid., 395.

74. Ibid., 390; emphasis mine.

75. Alexis de Tocqueville, *Democracy in America*, in *Democracy and Two Essays on America*, translated by Gerald E. Bevan (Penguin, 2003), 288.

76. Ibid.

77. Ibid., 298.

78. Richard Rorty, "Who Are We?: Moral Universalism and Economic Triage," *Diogenes* 44:1 (1996): 5–15.

79. Ibid., 8.

80. Rorty, "The Priority of Democracy to Philosophy," 177.

81. Rorty, "Who Are We?," 11–12.

82. Ibid.,12–13.

THE ABRAHAM DISTINCTION

1. Immanuel Kant, "An Answer to the Question: What Is Enlightenment?," translated by James Schmidt, in *What Is Enlightenment?:*

Eighteenth-Century Answers and Twentieth-Century Questions, translated by James Schmidt et al., edited by James Schmidt (University of California Press, 1996), 58.

2. Ibid., 58.

3. Benedictus de Spinoza, *Theological-Political Treatise*, translated by Michael Silverthorne and Jonathan Israel, edited by Jonathan Israel (Cambridge University Press, 2007), 13; emphasis mine.

4. Kant, "What Is Enlightenment?," 58.

5. Ibid., 59.

6. Ibid.

7. Ibid.

8. Henry D. Thoreau, "A Plea for Captain John Brown," in *Essays*, edited by Jeffery S. Cramer (Yale University Press, 2013), 213.

9. Moses Maimonides, *The Guide for the Perplexed*, translated by Shlomo Pines (University of Chicago Press, 1963), part 2, chapter 36.

10. Ibid.

11. Leo Strauss, *Spinoza's Critique of Religion*, translated by E. M. Sinclair (University of Chicago Press, 1997), 183. For a more thorough treatment of Maimonides's account of prophecy, which also considers its influence on Spinoza, see Heidi M. Ravven, "Some Thoughts on What Spinoza Learned from Maimonides About the Prophetic Imagination: Part 1. Maimonides on Prophecy and the Imagination," *Journal of the History of Philosophy* 39:2 (2001): 193–214. For a more recent treatment, see Ilaria Gaspari, "Immaginazione produttiva e profezia, fra Maimonide e Spinoza," *Teoria* 2 (2012): 169–97.

12. Shlomo Pines, translator's introduction, in Maimonides, *The Guide for the Perplexed*, lxxxix.

13. Jan Assmann, *The Price of Monotheism*, translated by Robert Savage (Stanford University Press, 2010).

14. Pines, translator's introduction, *The Guide for the Perplexed*, xxxii–i.

15. Exodus 33:20

16. Maimonides, *The Guide for the Perplexed*, introduction to the part 1.

17. Ibid., part 2, chapters 44–45.

18. Ibid., part 2, chapter 45.

19. Ibid.

20. Ibid.

21. Ibid. Emphasis mine

22. I'm unaware that Assmann or anyone else has made that suggestion, but such obedience could seem to follow quite naturally from the Mosaic distinction.

23. Genesis 22:1–2

24. Maimonides, *The Guide for the Perplexed*, part 1, chapter 2.

25. Ibid.

26. Genesis 3:5.

27. Maimonides, *The Guide for the Perplexed*, part 1, chapter 2. Emphasis mine

28. Ibid., part 3, chapter 24.

29. Ibid.

30. Sigmund Freud, *Moses and Monotheism*, translated by Katherine Jones (Hogarth Press and the Institute of Psycho-Analysis, 1939).

31. Genesis 22:2.

32. Ibid., 22:4.

33. Ibid., 22:5.

34. Ibid., 22:7.

35. Ibid., 22:7.

36. Ibid., 22:8.

37. Ibid., 22:9–19.

38. J. A. Emerton, "The Origin of the Promises to the Patriarchs in the Older Sources of the Book of Genesis," *Vetus Testamentum* 32:1 (1982): 18.

39. G. J. Wenham, *Genesis 16–50* (Word Books, 1994), 103.

40. Erich Auerbach, *Mimesis: The Representation of Reality in Western Literature*, translated by Willard R. Trask (Princeton University Press, 2003), 11.

41. Genesis 22:9–10.

42. Kant, *Critique of Judgment* (Hackett Publishing, 1987), *AA*, 5:260.

43. Immanuel Kant, *The Conflict of the Faculties*, translated by Mary J. Gregor (Orbis, 1979), 115n.

AFTERWORD

1. In one photo, another white person emerges in the frame, an "unidentified nun," as the caption reads.

2. Abraham Joshua Heschel, *The Prophets* (Harper & Row, 1962).

3. Abraham Joshua Heschel: "The Meaning of This War," in: *Moral Grandeur and Spiritual Audacity*, edited by Susannah Heschel (Farrar, Straus and Giroux 1996) pp. 209–212.

4. Martin Luther King Jr., "Beyond Vietnam: A Time to Break Silence," in *The Radical King*, edited by Cornel West (Beacon Press, 2015), 202.

5. Judith Butler, "The Compass of Mourning," *London Review of Books*, October 19, 2023. https://www.lrb.co.uk/the-paper/v45/n20/judith-butler/the-compass-of-mourning

6.   David Grossman, "Who Will We Be Once We Rise from the Ashes?" *Haaretz*, October 12 [Hebrew] https://www.haaretz.co.il/magazine/2023-10-12/ty-article-magazine/0000018b-1f97-d2fc-a59f-df9f22660000

THE OPPOSITE OF FORGETTING

1.   Yosef Hayim Yerushalmi, *Zakhor: Jewish History and Jewish Memory* (University of Washington Press, 1982).

2.   Herman Cohen, *Religion of Reason out of the Sources of Judaism* (Oxford, 1995), 446ff.

3.   Deuteronomy 25:17.

4.   Deuteronomy 25:19; 1 Samuel 15:3.

OMRI BOEHM is an associate professor and the chair of the Department of Philosophy at the New School for Social Research in New York City. He is the author of *Haifa Republic* (New York Review Books), *The Binding of Isaac: A Religious Model of Disobedience*, and *Kant's Critique of Spinoza*. His writings have appeared in *The New York Times*, *Die Zeit*, *El País*, and *Haaretz*, among other publications.